The Tale of the Greenlanders (II)
(The Tale of Einarr Sokkason)

Original Text, Translations, and Word Lists

Translated by
Matthew Leigh Embleton

Copyright ©2025 Matthew Leigh Embleton. All rights reserved.

The Tale of the Greenlanders (II) (The Tale of Einarr Sokkason)

The Tale of the Greenlanders (II) (The Tale of Einarr Sokkason) (*Old Norse*)............................4
Word List *(Old Norse to English)*..33
Word List *(English to Old Norse)* 49
The Tale of the Greenlanders (II) (The Tale of Einarr Sokkason) (*Old Icelandic*) 62
Word List *(Old Icelandic to English)*...91
Word List *(English to Old Icelandic)*...107
A Word Comparison of Old Norse and Old Icelandic Words 120

Cover: Old Norse text over an outline of Iceland. Author's design.

The original Old Norse and Old Icelandic texts are in the public domain.
These translations ©2022 Matthew Leigh Embleton
©2025 Matthew Leigh Embleton (This Edition)

Acknowledgments

I have long been fascinated by languages and history, and I am very grateful to the special people in my life who have supported and encouraged me in my work. Thank you for believing in me. You know who you are.

Introduction

Old Norse is a North Germanic language spoken by inhabitants of Scandinavia from about the 7th to the 15th centuries. Old Icelandic is a variety of Old West Norse that emerged during the Norse settlement of Iceland in the second half of the 9th century. The rich tradition of Icelandic literature survived by oral tradition over several centuries before being written down in the 13th Century. The Tale of the Greenlanders (II) (The Tale of Einarr Sokkason) (*Grœnlendinga þáttr (Einars þáttr Sokkasonar)*) is one of the many Tales of Icelanders or *Íslendingaþættir*. The word '*þáttr*' (plural: '*þættir*') translates as a strand of rope or a yarn, comparable to the word 'yarn' in English sometimes used to refer to a story.

This book contains:
- The Tale of the Greenlanders (II) (The Tale of Einarr Sokkason) (*Grœnlendinga þáttr (Einars þáttr Sokkasonar)*) (Old Norse Version)
- An Old Norse to English Word List
- An English to Old Norse Word List
- The Tale of the Greenlanders (II) (The Tale of Einarr Sokkason) (*Grœnlendinga þáttr (Einars þáttr Sokkasonar)*) (Old Icelandic Version)
- An Old Icelandic to English Word List
- An English to Old Icelandic Word List
- A Word Comparison of Old Norse and Old Icelandic words

The texts are presented in their original form, with a literal word-for-word line-by-line translation, and a Modern English translation, all side-by-side. In this way, it is possible to see and feel how the worked and how it has evolved. This book is designed to be of use and interest to anyone with a passion for the Old Norse or Old Icelandic language, Norse history, or languages and history in general.

The Tale of the Greenlanders (II) (The Tale of Einarr Sokkason) (*Old Norse*)

Old Norse	Literal	English
1	**1**	**1**
Sokki hét maðr ok var Þórisson.	Sokki was-named a-man and was Son-of-Thorri.	There was a man named Sokki, and he was the son of Thorri.
Hann bjó í Brattahlíð á Grænlandi.	He lived in Brattahlid in Greenland.	He lived in Brattahlid in Greenland.
Hann var mikils virðr ok vinsæll.	He was much respected and popular.	He was much respected and popular.
Einarr hét sonr hans ok var mannvænlegr maðr.	Einar was-named son his and was a-friendly man.	His son was named Einar and he was a friendly man.
Þeir feðgar áttu mikit vald á Grænlandi, ok váru þeir þar mjök fyrir mönnum.	They father-and-son had great power in Greenland, and were they there much foremost men.	The father and son had great power in Greenland and they were prominent men.
Einhverju sinni lét Sokki þings kveðja ok tjáði þat fyrir mönnum, at hann vildi, at landit væri eigi lengr byskupslaust, ok vildi, at allir landsmenn legði sína muni til, at byskupsstóll væri efldr.	One-occasion they had Sokki assembly called and voiced that before the-men, that he willed, that the-land be no longer bishop-less, and willed, that all lands-men put themselves should to, a bishop's-seat to-be strengthened.	On one occasion Sokki had an assembly called and announced before the men that he wished that the land should no longer be without a bishop, and he wished that all the men of the land should contribute towards a bishop's seat to be established.
Bændr játtuðu því allir.	Farmers agreed accordingly all.	Accordingly the farmers agreed to this.
Sokki bað Einar, son sinn, fara þessa ferð til Nóregs, kvað hann vera sendiligstan mann þess erendis at fara.	Sokki bid Einar, son his, travel this journey to Norway, said he would-be to-be-sent man this errand to travel.	Sokki asked his son Einar to travel on a journey to Norway as the best man for this errand.
Hann kveðst fara mundu, sem hann vildi.	He said travel would, as he willed.	He said that he would travel as wished.
Einarr hafði með sér tannvöru mikla ok svörð at heimta sik fram við höfðingja.	Einar had with him walrus-tusks great and skins to carry himself from with chieftains.	Einar had great walrus tusks and skins with him to further his case with the chieftains.

The Tale of the Greenlanders (II) (The Tale of Einarr Sokkason) (Old Norse)

Old Norse	Literal	English
Þeir kómu við Nóreg.	They came to Norway.	They came to Norway.
Þá var Sigurðr Jórsalafari konungr at Nóregi.	Then was Sigurd Jerusalem-Traveller the-king of Norway.	Then Sigurd Jerusalem-farer was king of Norway.
Einarr kom á fund konungs ok heimti sik fram með fégjöfum ok tjáði síðan mál sitt ok erendi ok beiddi konung þar til fulltings, at hann næði slíku sem hann beiddi fyrir nauðsyn landsins.	Einar came to meeting the-king's and presented himself from with fee-gifts and spoke then matters his and errand and bid the-king there to help, that he get such as he bid for needs the-lands.	Einar came to have a meeting with the king and presented himself well with wealthy gifts on account of his errand, and asked the king to help him get that which his lands needed.
Konungr lét þeim þat víst betr henta.	The-king had them that certainly better suitable.	The king agreed that it would certainly be better suited.
Síðan kallaði konungr til sín þann mann, er Arnaldr hét.	Then called the-king to him then a-man, was Arnald named.	Then the king called to him a man who was named Arnald.
Hann var góðr klerkr ok vel til kennimanns fallinn.	He was good cleric and well to teaching fallen.	He was a good cleric and well fallen to teaching.
Konungr beiddi, at hann réðist til þessa vanda fyrir guðs sakir ok bænar hans, "ok mun ek senda þik til Danmarkar á fund Özurar erkibyskups í Lundi með mínum bréfum ok innsiglum".	The-king bid, that he deal to this problem for god's sake and prayers his, "and will I send you to Denmark to meet Ossur archbishop in Lund with my briefs and seals".	The king asked him to deal with this problem God's sake and his prayers, "And I will send you to Denmark to meet archbishop Ossur of Lund with my letters and seals".
Arnaldr kvaðst ófúss til at ráðast, fyrst fyrir sjálfs síns sakar, er hann væri lítt til fallinn, ok síðan at skilja við vini sína ok frændr, í þriðja stað at eiga við torsóttligt fólk.	Arnald said reluctant to that arrange, firstly for himself his sake, as he was little to weak, and then to part with friends his and kinsmen, and thirdly stand to not with difficult folk.	Arnald said that he was reluctant to arrange this, firstly for his sake because he was ill-fitted for it, and secondly to part with his friends and kinsmen, and thirdly he did not wish to have to talk to such difficult folk.
Konungr kvað hann því meira gott mundu eftir taka sem hann hefði meiri skapraun af mönnum.	The-king said he that more good would afterwards take as he had more temperament of men.	The king said that the more his difficulty at the hands of temperamental men, the greater his reward would be afterwards.

The Tale of the Greenlanders (II) (The Tale of Einarr Sokkason) (Old Norse)

Old Norse	Literal	English
Hann kveðst eigi nenna at skerast undan hans bæn, "en ef þess verðr auðit, at ek taka byskupsvígslu, þá vil ek, at Einarr sveri mér þess eið at halda ok fulltingja rétt byskupsstólsins ok eignum þeim, er guði eru gefnar, ok hegna þeim, er á ganga, ok sé varnarmaðr fyrir öllum hlutum staðarins".	He said not bothered to cutting away-from his prayers, "but if this becomes possible, that I take bishop's-appointment, then will I, that Einar swear to-me this oath to hold and fulfil rights bishop's-seat and owning them, the priest are given, and protected they, are to go, and being defender for all things the-place".	He said that he did not want the bother of cutting away from his prayers "but if it becomes possible that I take the appointment of bishop, then I wish Einar to swear to me this oath, to hold and fulfil the rights of the bishop's seat, and all that is given to the priest, and to be the protector and defender of all things to do with the bishop's seat".
Konungr kvað hann þat gera skyldu.	The-king said he that to-do should.	The king said that he should do this.
Einarr kvaðst mundu undir þat ganga.	Einar said would submit to go.	Einar said he would submit to going along with it.
Síðan fór byskupsefni á fund Özurar erkibyskups ok sagði honum sitt erendi með konungsbréfum.	Then travelled the-bishop-elect to meet Ossur archbishop and said to-him this errand with the-king's-brief.	Then the bishop-elect went to meet archbishop Ossur and told him of his errand with the king's letters.
Erkibyskup tók honum vel, ok reyndust hugi við.	The-archbishop took him well, and gave-him his-mind with.	The archbishop received him well and gave to him with his mind.
Ok er byskup sá, at þessi maðr var vel til tignar fallinn, vígði hann Arnald til byskups ok leysti hann vel af hendi.	And when the-bishop saw, that this man was well to position fallen, consecrated he Arnald to bishop and released him well of hand.	And when the bishop saw that this man was well given to the position he consecrated Arnald to bishop and parted with him warmly.
Síðan kom Arnaldr byskup til konungs, ok tók hann við honum vel.	Then came Arnald bishop to the-king, and took he with him well.	Then bishop Arnald went to the king and he received him well.
Einarr hafði haft með sér bjarndýri af Grænlandi ok gaf þat Sigurði konungi.	Einar had had with him a-bear from Greenland and gave it Sigurd the-king.	Einar had a bear with him from Greenland and gave it to Sigurd the king.
Fékk hann þar í mót sæmðir ok metorð af konungi.	Got he then to meet honour and esteem from the-king.	He then got honour and esteem from the king.
Síðan fóru þeir á einu skipi, byskup ok Einarr.	Then travelled they on one ship, the-bishop and Einar.	Then they travelled on a ship, the bishop and Einar.

The Tale of the Greenlanders (II) (The Tale of Einarr Sokkason) (Old Norse)

Old Norse	Literal	English
Á öðru skipi bjóst Arnbjörn Austmaðr ok norrænir menn með honum ok vildu ok fara út til Grænlands.	On another ship prepared Arnbjorn Eastern-man and Nordic men with him and willed also travel out to Greenland.	Prepared on another ship was Arnbjorn the Norwegian and other Norse men with him who wished to travel to Greenland.
Síðan létu þeir í haf, ok greiðist eigi byrrinn mjök í hag þeim, ok kómu þeir byskup ok Einarr í Holtavatnsós undir Eyjafjöllum á Íslandi.	Then had they to sea, and paying not bearing much of circumstances theirs, and came they bishop and Einar to Holtavatnsos under Eyjafjolls in Iceland.	Then they put to sea and the situation was not very favourable for them, and the bishop and Einar arrived in Holtavatnsós under the Eyjafjolls in Iceland.
Þá bjó Sæmundur inn fróði í Odda.	Then lived Saemund the learned in Odda.	Then Saemund the learned lived in Odda.
Hann fór á fund byskups ok bauð honum til sín um vetrinn.	He went to meet the-bishop and invited him to his about winter.	He went to see the bishop and invited him to stay with him for the winter.
Byskup þakkaði honum ok lézt þat þiggja mundu.	Bishop thanked him and had that accepted would.	The bishop thanked him and had accepted it.
Einarr var undir Eyjafjöllum um vetrinn.	Einar was under Eyjafjolls about winter.	Einar was under Eyjafjolls during the winter.
Þat er sagt, þá er byskup reið frá skipi ok menn hans, at þeir áðu á bæ nökkurum í Landeyjum ok sátu úti.	It is said, when that bishop rode from the-ship and men his, that they that to a-farm some in The-Landeys and sat outside.	It is said that when the bishop and his men got off the ship, they went to a farm in the Landeys and sat outside.
Þá gekk út kerling ein ok hafði ullkamb í hendi.	Then went out old-woman one and had wool-comb in hand.	Then an old woman walked out alone with a wool comb in her hand.
Hún gekk at einum manni ok mælti:	She went to one man and said:	She walked up to one man and said:
"Muntu festa, bokki, tindinn í kambi mínum?"	"Shall-you fix, buck, pin in comb mine?"	"Will you fix the pin in my comb, buck?"
Hann tók við ok kvaðst mundu at gera ok tók hnjóðhamar ór mal einum ok gerði at, ok líkaði kerlingu allvel.	He took with and said would to done and took hammer out-of the-matter one and did it, and liked the-old-woman all-well.	He took it over and said that he would do it, and he took a hammer off the ground and did it, and the old woman liked this very well,
En þat var byskup raunar,	And it was a-bishop actually,	and it was actually a bishop.

The Tale of the Greenlanders (II) (The Tale of Einarr Sokkason) (Old Norse)

Old Norse	Literal	English
hann var hagr vel, ok er því frá þessu sagt, at hann sýndi lítillæti sitt.	he was handy well, and was therefore from this said, that he showed humility his.	He was very handy and it is told from this of how he showed his humility.
Hann var í Odda um vetrinn, ok fór með þeim Sæmundi allvel.	He was in Odda about winter, and went with them Saemund all-well.	He was in Odda during the winter and got on very well with Saemund.
En til þeira Arnbjarnar spurðist ekki.	But to them Arnbjarn heard-of not.	But they did not hear of Arnbjarn.
Ætluðu þeir byskup, at hann mundi kominn til Grænlands.	Supposed they bishop, that he would come to Greenland.	They thought the bishop would come to Greenland.
Um sumarit eftir fóru þeir byskup ok Einarr af Íslandi ok kómu við Grænland í Eiríksfjörð, ok tóku menn við þeim allvel.	About summer after went they the-bishop and Einar from Iceland and came to Greenland in Eriksfjord, and took men with them all-well.	In the following summer, the bishop and Einar left Iceland and arrived at Greenland in Eriksfjord and were well received by the people.
Spurðu þeir þá enn ekki til Arnbjarnar, ok þótti þat undarligt, ok liðu svá nökkur sumur.	Heard-of they then but not to Arnbjarn, and thought that strange, and passed so some summers.	They still didn't hear about Arnbjarn and thought it was strange, and then a few summers passed.
Gerðist nú umræða mikil, at þeir muni týnzt hafa.	Became now discussed much, that they would lost have.	There was now much discussion that they must have been lost.
Byskup setti stól sinn í Görðum ok réðst þangat til.	Bishop set seat his in Gardar and ruled from-then to.	The bishop placed his chair in Gardar and ruled until then.
Var Einarr honum þá mestr styrkðarmaðr ok þeir feðgar.	Was Einar to-him then the-most supporter and they father-and-son.	Einar was his greatest supporter then, and they were father and son.
Þeir váru ok mest metnir af öllum landsmönnum af byskupi.	They were and most important of all lands-men of the-bishop.	They were and the most valued of all the countrymen by the bishop.

2

Sigurðr hét maðr ok var Njálsson, grænlenzkr maðr.	Sigurd was-named a-man and was Son-of-Njal, a-Greenlander man.	There was a man named Sigurd who was the son of Njal, a Greenlander man.
Hann fór oft á haustum til fangs í óbyggðir.	He travelled often out autumn to captivity in un-settled.	He often went in the fall to captivity in the wilderness.

The Tale of the Greenlanders (II) (The Tale of Einarr Sokkason) (Old Norse)

Old Norse	Literal	English
Hann var sægarpr mikill.	He was sea-champion much.	He was very much a champion of the sea.
Þeir váru fimmtán saman.	They were fifteen altogether.	There were fifteen of them together.
Þeir kómu um sumarit at jöklinum Hvítserk ok höfðu fundit nökkurar eldstóar manna ok enn nökkurn veiðiskap.	They came about summer to a-glacier Hvitserk and had-they found some fire-place men and still some hunting.	They came in the summer to the glacier Hvitserk and had found several small groups of men and still some hunting.
Þá mælti Sigurðr:	Then spoke Sigurd:	Then Sigurd said:
"Hvárs eruð þér fúsari, at hverfa aftr eða fara lengra?	"Which are you willing, to turn back or travel longer?	"Which are you more willing to go back or go further?
Er nú ekki sumars mikit eftir, en fang orðit lítit".	Is now not summer much remaining, but resources have-become little".	There isn't much left of the summer now, but the catch has become short".
Hásetar kváðust fúsari aftr at hverfa ok sögðu mannhættu mikla at fara um stórfjörðu undir jöklum.	The-crew said willing back to turn and said dangerous much to travel about large-fjords under glaciers.	The crew said they were more willing to turn back and said that it was very dangerous to go through a large fjord under glaciers.
Hann kvað þat satt, "en svá segir mér hugr um, at eftir muni it meira fangit, ef því nái".	He said that true, "but so says to-me mind about, that later would then more to-catch, if then getting".	He said it was true "but then my mind tells me that later the more will be caught if it is possible".
Þeir báðu hann ráða, kváðust lengi hans forsjá hlítt hafa ok þó vel gefizt.	They asked him advice, said long his foresight satisfactory had and though well given.	They asked him for advice, saying that they had been under his guardianship for a long time and that it had been successful.
Honum kveðst meira um at halda fram, ok svá var gert.	He said more about that to-hold from, and so was done.	He said that there was more to claim, and so it was done.
Steinþórr hét maðr, er á skipi þeira var.	Steinthor was-named a-man, was on ship theirs was.	A man on their ship was called Steinthor.
Hann tók til orða:	He took to words:	He spoke:
"Dreymði mik í nótt, Sigurðr",	"Dreamed me about the-night, Sigurd",	"I had a dream last night, Sigurd",

The Tale of the Greenlanders (II) (The Tale of Einarr Sokkason) (Old Norse)

Old Norse	Literal	English
sagði hann, "ok mun ek segja þér drauminn.	said he, "and will I say to-you the-dream.	he said, "and I will tell you the dream
Nú	Now	Now
er vér fórum á fjörðinn þennan inn mikla, þóttumst ek kominn í milli bjarga nökkurra ok æpa til bjargar mér".	when we travel to fjord then the much, thought I coming in between rescuing something and shouting to rescue me".	when we went to this great fjord, I thought I came between something to be rescued from, and shouting for my rescue".
Sigurðr kvað draum meðallagi góðan, "ok skyldir þú þar eigi björg undir fótum troða ok hitta eigi í þann einangr, at þú mættir eigi munni halda".	Sigurd said dream moderately good, "and should you there not rocks under feet tread and find not in that alone-going, that you might not mouth hold".	Sigurd said it was a moderately good dream "and you should not trample rocks under your feet there and you should not find yourself so alone that you could not keep your mouth shut".
Steinþórr var heldr æðimaðr í skaplyndi ok óforsjáll.	Steinthor was rather of-mind in temper and impulsive.	Steinthor was rather a hot-tempered and impulsive person.
Ok er þeir sækja inn á fjörðinn, þá mælti Sigurðr:	And when they sought in the fjord, then spoke Sigurd:	And when they entered the fjord, Sigurd said:
"Hvárt er sem mér sýnist, at skip sé inn á fjörðinn?"	"Whether is as to-me seems, that ship this in the fjord?"	"Does it seem to me that a ship is in the fjord?"
Þeir kváðu svá vera.	They said so being.	They said it was so.
Sigurðr kvað þat tíðendum mundu gegna,	Sigurd said that news would pass,	Sigurd said that this would bring great news.
heldu nú síðan inn at ok sá, at skipit var sett upp í einn árós ok gert fyrir ofan.	held now then in to and saw, the ship was sat up in a river-mouth and made for above.	Now they went inward and saw that the ship was set up in one estuary and made covered.
Þat var mikit hafskip.	It was a-great sea-going-ship.	It was a great sea-going ship.
Síðan gengu þeir á land ok sá skála ok tjald skammt frá.	Then went they to land and saw cabin and tent a-short-distance from.	Then they went ashore and saw a cabin and a tent nearby.
Þá mælti Sigurðr, at þeir mundu tjalda fyrst, "ok er nú liðit á dag, ok vil ek, at menn sé kyrrlátir ok varúðgir".	Then spoke Sigurd, that they would tent-up first, "and is now passed in the-day, and wish I, that men are still and cautious".	Then Sigurd said that they would camp first "and now it's late in the day and I want people to be quiet and careful".
Ok svá gerðu þeir.	And so done was.	And so it was done.

The Tale of the Greenlanders (II) (The Tale of Einarr Sokkason) (Old Norse)

Old Norse	Literal	English
Ok um morgininn ganga þeir ok sjást um.	And about morning went they and looked about.	And in the morning they went and looked about.
Þeir sjá stokk einn hjá sér, ok stóð í bolöx ok mannshræ hjá.	They saw a-log one beside them, and stood in the-trunk and human-body beside.	They saw a log by them and an axe in the butt and a human carcass.
Sigurðr kvað þann mann viðinn höggvit hafa ok hafa orðit vanmeginn af megri.	Sigurd said that the-man the-trees struck had and had become weak of meagre.	Sigurd said that the man had been striking trees and had become weak from hunger.
Síðan gengu þeir at skálanum ok sá þar annat mannshræ.	Then went they to the-cabin and saw there another dead-body.	Then they walked to the cabin and saw another corpse there.
Sigurðr kvað þann gengit hafa, meðan hann mátti, "ok munu þessir verit hafa þjónustumenn þeira, er í skálanum eru".	Sigurd said then walked had, as-long-as he might, "and would these been have servants-of they, who about the-cabin were".	Sigurd said that he had walked for as long as he could "and these will be the servants of who are in the cabin".
Öx lá ok hjá þessum.	Axe lay also beside these.	An axe lay beside these.
Þá mælti Sigurðr:	Then spoke Sigurd:	Then Sigurd said:
"Þat kalla ek ráð at rjúfa skálann ok láta leggja út daun af líkum þeim, er inni eru, ok yldu, er lengi munu legit hafa,	"It call I decide to break-open the-hut and lay-out have out the-dead of bodies they, who in were, and decay, are long may laid have,	"This I call our plan, to break open the cabin and let the stench of the dead out, for the corpses will have been lying there for a long time.
ok varist menn fyrir at verða, því at þess er eigi lítil ván, at mönnum verði at því mein, er mjök er á mót eðli manna, þótt líkendi sé á því, at menn þessir muni oss ekki illt gera".	and weariness men for that be, because that this is not little hope, that men be that because-of disease, and much is to meet nature man's, though alike they-are that they, the men these should to-us not ill be-done".	And men be wary of it, because there is nothing more certain than men will be harmed by it, and it is very against human wellbeing, and though there are similarities, these men will not harm us".
Steinþórr kvað slíkt undarligt, at gera sér meira fyrir en þyrfti, ok gekk á hurðina, en þeir rufu skálann.	Steinthor said such strange, to do as more for than needed, and went to the-door, but they broke-up the-cabin.	Steinthor said that it was such a strange thing to do more than was necessary, and went to the door as they broke open the cabin.
Ok er Steinþórr gekk út, leit Sigurðr til hans ok mælti:	And when Steinthor went out, looked Sigurd to him and said:	And when Steinthor came out Sigurd got a look at him and said:

The Tale of the Greenlanders (II) (The Tale of Einarr Sokkason) (Old Norse)

Old Norse	Literal	English
"Allmjök er manninum brugðit".	"All-great is this-man upset".	"This man is greatly upset".
Hann tók þegar at æpa ok hlaupa, en þeir eftir félagar hans.	He took straightaway to shouting and running, but they followed companions his.	He started shouting and running away, but his companions followed him.
Hann hleypr síðan í hamarrifu nökkura, þar er engi mátti at honum komast, ok þar fekk hann bana.	He ran then into crags some, there where no-one might to him come, and there got he death.	He ran into some crags and became stuck between them so that no-one could get to him, and there he died.
Sigurðr kvað hann of berdreyman.	Sigurd said he of clear-dreams.	Sigurd said his dream was clearly true.
Síðan rufu þeir skálann ok gerðu eftir því, sem Sigurðr mælti, ok varð þeim ekki mein at.	Then tore-up they the-cabin and did following according, as Sigurd said, and came to-them not harm by.	Then they tore up the cabin and followed accordingly as Sigurd had told them, and no harm came to them.
Þeir sá þar í skálanum menn dauða ok fé mikit.	They saw there in the-cabin men dead and wealth much.	They saw dead people and a lot of money in the cabin.
Þá mælti Sigurðr:	Then said Sigurd:	Then Sigurd said:
"Þat sýnist mér ráð, at þér hleypið holdi af beinum þeira í heitukötlum þeira, er þeir hafa átt, ok er svá hægra til kirkju at færa.	"That seems to-me advisable, that you discharge flesh off bones theirs in boiling-cauldrons theirs, that they had had, and then so right to the-church to bring.	"It seems to me advisable that you get the flesh off their bones in their hot cauldrons that they have, and then move them to church.
Ok er þat líkast, at Arnbjörn muni hér verit hafa, því at skip þetta annat it fagra, er hér stendr á landi, hefi ek heyrt, at hann hafi átt".	And is that likely, that Arnbjorn should here been has, because that ship this other then the-fairest, is here standing about the-land, have I heard, that he had had".	And it seems likely that Arnbjorn will have been here, because this ship is one of the most beautiful that is standing on this land, I have heard that he had".
Þat var höfðaskip ok steint ok mikil gersemi.	It was a-headed-ship and stone-carving and much treasure.	It was a ship with a figurehead and stone-carving and great treasure.
Kaupskipit var brotit mjök neðan, ok kvaðst Sigurðr ætla, at þat mundi at engum nytjum verða.	Merchant-ship was broken much below, and said Sigurd suppose, that it would to no use be.	The merchant ship was broken below, and Sigurd said that it would be of no use.

The Tale of the Greenlanders (II) (The Tale of Einarr Sokkason) (Old Norse)

Old Norse	Literal	English
Þeir taka ór sauminn, en brenndu skipit ok höfðu hlaðna ferjuna ór óbyggðum, eftirbátinn ok höfðaskipit.	They took out-from the-seam, and burned the-ship and had loaded the-ferry out-of the-unsettled-land, the-after-boat and head-ship.	They took out everything from the seams and burned the ship and had loaded to ferry out of the unsettled land, the second boat, and the head ship.
Þeir kómu í byggðina ok fundu byskup í Görðum, ok sagði Sigurðr honum tíðendin ok fjárfundinn.	They came to the-settlement and found bishop in Gardar, and said Sigurd to-him the-news and wealth-finding.	They came to the settlement and found the bishop at Gardar, and Sigurd told him the news and of finding the wealth.
"Nú kann ek eigi annat at sjá",	"Now can I not anything-else to see",	"Now I can't see anything else",
sagði hann, "en þat fé þeira muni bezt komit, er beinum þeira fylgir, ok ef ek á á nökkuru ráð, þá vil ek, at svá sé".	said he, "but that wealth theirs would best come, that bones theirs followed, and if I of of some advice, then wish I, to so to-be".	he said, "but their money will be best served if their placed with their bones, and if I have any say, I want it to be so".
Byskup kvað hann vel hafa með farit ok vitrliga, ok þat mæltu allir.	Bishop said he well had with going and wise-like, and that said all.	The bishop said he had acted well and wisely, and everyone said so.
Mikit fé fylgði líkum þeira.	Much wealth followed bodies theirs.	A lot of money followed their corpses.
Byskup kvað gersemi mikla vera höfðaskipit.	Bishop said treasure much being head-ship.	The bishop said the great treasure was the head ship.
Sigurðr kvað ok þat sannligast, at þat færi til staðarins fyrir sálum þeira.	Sigurd said and it truthfully, that it going to the-place for souls theirs.	Sigurd said, and most truly, that it would go to the bishop's seat for the good of their souls.
Öðru fé skiptu þeir með sér, er fundit höfðu, at grænlenzkum lögum.	Other wealth divided they with themselves, as found had, to Greenlandic law.	They shared the other money they had found according to Greenlandic law.
Ok er þessi tíðendi kómu til Nóregs, þá spurði þat sá maðr, er Özurr hét ok var systursonr Arnbjarnar.	And when these tidings came to Norway, then learned that so man, was Ossur named and was sister's-son Arnbjarnar.	And when these tidings came to Norway, the man whose name was Ossur, who was Arnbjorn's sister's son, learned about it.
Ok	And	...and
fleiri menn váru þeir, er sína frændr höfðu misst á því skipi ok væntu til greiðslu um féit.	more men were they, in their kinsman had lost to because the-ship and expected to compensation about wealth.	there were more men on the ship that had lost their cousins and were expecting payment for the money.

The Tale of the Greenlanders (II) (The Tale of Einarr Sokkason) (Old Norse)

Old Norse	Literal	English
Þeir kómu í Eiríksfjörð, ok sóttu menn til fundar við þá ok slógu kaupum.	They came to Eriksfjord, and sought men to meet with then and strike a-deal.	They came to Eriksfjord and fetched people to meet them and make a deal.
Síðan tóku menn sér vistir.	Then took men themselves supplies.	Then people took supplies.
Özurr stýrimaðr fór í Garða til byskups ok var þar um vetrinn.	Ossur steersman went to Gardar to the-bishop and was there about winter.	Ossur the steersman went to Gardar to see the bishop and stayed there during the winter.
Í Vestribyggð var þá annat kaupskip.	In Vestribyggd was then another merchant-ship.	In the Western Settlement there was another merchant ship then.
Þar var Kolbeinn Þorljótsson, norrænn maðr.	There was Kolbein Son-of-Thorljot, Nordic man.	There was Kolbein Son-of-Thorljot, a Nordic man.
Inu þriðja skipi réð sá maðr, er Hermundr hét ok var Koðránsson, ok Þorgils, bróðir hans ok höfðu mikla sveit manna.	The third ship commanded so man, was Hermund named and was Son-of-Kodran, and Thorgils, brother his and had much company of-men.	The third ship was commanded by a man named Hermund, who was the son of Kodran, and his brother Thorgils, and they had a large force of men.

3

Um vetrinn kom Özurr at máli við byskup, at hann ætti þangat féván eftir Arnbjörn, frænda sinn, ok beiddi byskup þar gera greiða á bæði fyrir sína hönd ok annarra manna.	About winter came Ossur to discuss with the-bishop, that he had from-there fee-trust after Arnbjorn, kinsman his, and bid bishop there to-give assistance as asked for his hand and other men.	During the winter, Ossur discussed with the bishop that he had a trust there for his uncle Arnbjorn and asked the bishop there to give assistance both on his behalf and on other people's behalf.
Byskup kvaðst fé tekit hafa eftir grænlenzkum lögum eftir slíka atburði, kvaðst þetta ekki gert hafa með einræði sitt, kvað þat makligast, at þat fé færi þeim til sáluhjápar, er aflat höfðu, ok til þeirar kirkju, er bein þeira váru at grafin, sagði þat manndómsleysi at kalla nú til fjár þess.	The-bishop said wealth taken had after Greenlandic law after such events, said it not made had with self-will this, said that most, that it wealth go-to them to souls, who gain had, and to their church, where bones theirs were to in-the-grave, said that meanness to claim now to money this.	The bishop said that he had taken money according to Greenlandic laws after such events, he said that he had not done this with his decision-making, he said that it was most appropriate that the money should go to the souls they had earned and to the church where their bones were buried, he said it was mean to claim now to this money.

The Tale of the Greenlanders (II) (The Tale of Einarr Sokkason) (Old Norse)

Old Norse	Literal	English
Síðan vildi Özurr eigi vera í Görðum með byskupi ok fór til sveitunga sinna, ok héldu sik svá allir samt um vetrinn.	Then willed Ossur not to-be at Gardar with the-bishop and went to men-company his, and held him so all-the-same about winter.	After that, Ossur did not want to stay in Gardar with the bishop and went to his companions, and they all stayed the winter anyway.
Um várit bjó Özurr mál til þings þeira Grænlendinga, ok var þat þing í Görðum.	About spring prepared Ossur a-case to the-assembly theirs Greenlanders, and was it assembly in Gardar.	In the spring, Ossur prepared a case for the assembly of the Greenlanders, and that meeting was held in Gardar.
Kom þar byskup ok Einarr Sokkason, ok höfðu þeir fjölmenni mikit.	Came there bishop and Einar Son-of-Sokki, and had they following-men many.	Bishop and Einar Sokkason came there and they had a lot of followers.
Özurr kom þar ok þeir skipverjar hans.	Ossur came there and they crew his.	Ossur and his crew arrived there.
Ok er dómr var settr, þá gekk Einarr at dómi með fjölmenni ok kveðst ætla, at þeim mundi erfitt at eiga við útlenda menn í Nóregi, ef svá skyldi þar.	And when judgement was set, then went Einar to the-court with many-people and said supposed, to them would difficult to have with foreign men in Norway, if so should there.	And when the sentence was passed, Einar went to the court with many people and said that they would find it difficult to deal with foreigners in Norway if it happened there.
"Viljum vér þau lög hafa, er hér ganga",	"Wish we then law have, that here going",	"We wish to have the law that goes here",
sagði Einarr.	said Einar.	said Einar.
Ok er dómrinn fór út, náðu Austmenn eigi málum fram at koma ok stukku frá.	And when the-judgement went out, reached Eastern-men not case from to come and went-away from.	And when the judgement came out, the Eastern-men could not progress forward and went away.
Nú líkar Özuri illa, þykkist hafa af óvirðing, en fé ekki, ok varð þat hans órræði, at hann ferr til, þar er skipit er þat it steinda, ok hjó ór tvau borð, sínu megin hvárt, upp frá kilinum.	Now likes Ossur ill, seems have of un-worthy, but wealth not, and became it his solution, that he went to, there where the-ship was that the stone-one, and struck out-of two boards, theirs sides each, up from the-keel.	Now Ossur did not like this and thought ill of it, because of the disrespect not the money, and so became his solution, that he went to where the ship was that had the stone and struck out two boards, one on each side, upwards from the keel.
Eftir þat fór hann til Vestribyggðar ok hitti þá Kolbein ok Ketil Kálfsson ok sagði þeim svá búit.	After that went he to Vestribyggd and met then Kolbein and Ketil Son-of-Kalf and said to-them so settled.	After that he went to Vestribyggd (The-Western-Settlement) and met Kolbein and Ketil Kalfsson and told them it was over.

The Tale of the Greenlanders (II) (The Tale of Einarr Sokkason) (Old Norse)

Old Norse	Literal	English
Kolbeinn kvað ósæmð til tekna, enda sagði hann órræðit ekki gott.	Kolbein said dishonourable to taken, and said he solution not good.	Kolbein said that it was taken as dishonourable and that the solution was not good.
Ketill mælti:	Ketil said:	Ketil said:
"Fýsa vil ek þik, at þú ráðist hingat til vár, því at ek hefi spurt fastmæli byskups ok Einars, en þú munt vanfærr at sitja fyrir tilstilli byskups, en framkvæmð Einars, ok verum heldr allir saman".	"Desire will I you, that you advise here until spring, because that I have learned opinion the-bishop's and Einar's, but you would unable to sit through guidance the-bishop's, but execution Einar's, and we rather all together".	"I want you to come here until spring, because I have learned the bishop's and Einar's opinion, and you will be unable to sit through the bishop's guidance, and Einar's actions and we should rather all stand together".
Hann kvað ok líkligast, at þat mundi af ráðast.	He said and likely, that it would of be-arranged.	He said that it was so, and it would likely be arranged.
Þar var í sveit með þeim kaupmönnum Ísa-Steingrímr.	There was in the-company with them trading-men Isa-Steingrim.	There was in the company of merchants with them a man named Isa-Steingrim.
Özurr fór þá aftr til Kiðjabergs.	Ossur went then back to Kidjaberg.	Ossur then went back to Kidjaberg.
Þar hafði hann áðr verit.	There had he before been.	He had been there before.

4

Byskup varð reiðr mjök, er hann spurði, at spillt var skipinu, ok kallar til sín Einar Sokkason ok mælti:	Bishop became angry much, when he learned, that damaged was the-ship, and called to him Einar Son-of-Sokki and said:	The Bishop became very-much angry when he learned of the damage that was done to the ship, and called Einar Sokkason before him and said:
"Nú er til þess at taka, er þú hézt með svardaga, er vér fórum af Nóregi, at refsa svívirðing staðarins ok hans eigna við þá, er þat gerðu.	"Now it to this that take, what you promised with oath, was we travelled from Norway, to punish disgrace of-the-place and its property with then, is it to-do.	"Now it is for you to take action as you promised by oath when we travelled from Norway, to punish the disgrace to this place and its property and those who did it.
Nú kalla ek Özurr hafa fyrirgert sér, er hann hefir spillt eign várri ok sýnt oss í öllum hlutum ópekkðarsvip.	Now call I Ossur have before-done himself, as he has damaged property ours and shown us to ill things ungraceful.	Now I announce that Ossur's life is forfeit, as he has damaged our property and shown us the most disgraceful ill.

The Tale of the Greenlanders (II) (The Tale of Einarr Sokkason) (Old Norse)

Old Norse	Literal	English
Nú er ekki at dyljast við, at mér líkar eigi svá búit ok ek kalla þik eiðrofa, ef kyrrt er".	Now is none to hiding with, that to-me like not so settled and I call you breach-of-oath, if still are".	Now there is no hiding that I do not like things as they so are, and I will call you in breach of oath if they still are".
Einarr svarar:	Einar answered:	Einar answered:
"Eigi er þetta vel gert, herra, en mæla munu þat sumir, at nökkur várkunn sé á við Özur, svá miklu sem hann er sviptr, þótt eigi sé vel í höndum haft, þá er þeir sá góða gripi, er frændr þeira höfðu átt, ok náðu eigi,	"Not is this well done, sir, but badly would that some, that some pity is to with Ossur, so much as he is deprived, though not is well in handling has, then is they saw good treasure, that kinsmen theirs had owned, and reached not,	"This is not a good thing to have done sir, but it would be bad for some may pity Ossur, for he has been deprived of so much, and it will not be handled well if they saw the good treasure that their kinsmen had owned and were unable to obtain it.
ok veit ek varla, hverju ek skal hér um heita".	and knowing I hardly, how I shall here about be-called".	And I hardly know how I shall call this.
Þeir skilðu fáliga, ok var reiðisvipr á byskupi.	They parted coolly, and was angry of the-bishop.	They parted coolly, and the bishop looked angry.
Ok þá er menn sóttu til kirkjumessu ok til veizlu á Langanes, var byskup þar ok Einarr at veizlunni.	And then when men sought to church-mass and to feast at Langanes, was the-bishop there and Einar at the-feast.	And when people went to church mass and to a feast at Langanes, the bishop was there and Einar was at the feast.
Margt fólk var komit til tíða, ok söng byskup messu.	Many folk were come to the-service, and sang the-bishop mass.	Many people had come and the bishop sang mass.
Þar var kominn Özurr ok stóð undir kirkju sunnan ok við kirkjuvegginn, ok talaði sá maðr við hann, er Brandr hét ok var Þórðarson, heimamaðr byskups.	There was come Ossur and standing under the-church to-the-south and with church-wall, and told so man with him, was Brand named and was Son-of-Thord, house-man the-bishop's.	Ossur had arrived there and was standing under the church to the south and by the church wall, and talking to the man with him whose name was Brand Thorisson, the bishop's houseman.
Þessi maðr bað Özur vægja til við byskup, "ok vænti ek",	This man bid Ossur make-peace to with the-bishop, "and expect I",	This man asked Ossur to make peace with the bishop, "and I expect",
sagði hann, "at þá muni vel duga, en nú agir við svá".	said he, "that then would well aided, but not desirable with so".	he said, "that all will be well, but it is not desirable as it is".

The Tale of the Greenlanders (II) (The Tale of Einarr Sokkason) (Old Norse)

Old Norse	Literal	English
Özurr kvaðst ekki fá þat af sér, svá illa sem við hann var búit,	Ossur said not get that of him, so ill as with he was settled,	Ossur said that he could not because of the ill with which it had been concluded.
ok áttu þeir nú um þetta at tala.	and have they now about this to spoke.	And they now spoke about this.
Þá gengu þeir byskup frá kirkju ok heim til húsa, ok var Einarr þar í göngu.	Then went they the-bishop from the-church and home to house, and was Einar there in going.	Then the bishop and the others went from the church to the house, and Einar went along.
Ok er þeir kómu fyrir skáladyrrnar, þá snerist Einarr frá fylgðinni ok gekk einn í brott til kirkjugarðsins ok tók öxi ór hendi tíðamanni einum ok gekk suðr um kirkjuna.	And as they came before the-door, then turned Einar from following and went alone to away to churchyard and took axe out-of hand worshippers one and went south around the-church.	And as they came to the door then Einar turned away from the followers and went away alone to the churchyard and took an axe out of the hand of one of the worshippers and went around to the south side of the church.
Özurr stóð þar ok studdist á öxi sína.	Ossur stood there and stood on axe his.	Ossur stood there leaning on his axe.
Einarr hjó hann þegar banahögg ok gekk inn eftir þat, ok váru þá borð uppi.	Einar struck him straight-away death-blow and went in after that, and were then the-tables up.	Einar struck him a death blow straight away and went inside by which time the tables were up.
Einarr steig undir borðit gegnt byskupi ok mælti ekki orð.	Einar stepped under the-table opposite the-bishop and spoke not a-word.	Einar took his seat at the table opposite the bishop and spoke not a word.
Síðan gekk hann Brandr Þórðarson í stofuna ok fyrir byskup ok mælti:	Then went he Brand Son-of-Thord in sitting-room and before bishop and said:	Then Brand Thordarson went into the sitting room before the bishop and said:
"Er nökkut tíðenda sagt yðr, herra?"	"Is some news told you, sir?"	"Has some news been told to you sir?"
Byskup kvaðst ekki spurt hafa, "eða hvat segir þú?"	Bishop said not learned had, "but what say you?"	The bishop said he had not heard "but what say you?"
Hann svarar:	He answered:	He answered:
"Sígast lét nú einn hér úti".	"Sinking laid now one here outside".	"Someone has dropped down laying dead here outside".
Byskup mælti:	Bishop spoke:	The bishop said:

The Tale of the Greenlanders (II) (The Tale of Einarr Sokkason) (Old Norse)

Old Norse	Literal	English
"Hverr veldr því, eða hverr er fyrir orðinn?"	"Who caused therefore, or who is before the-words?"	"Who causes it or who is behind the word?"
Brandr kvað þann nær, er frá kunni at segja.	Brand said then as-far, as from known to say.	Brand said someone as far away as him knew to say.
Byskup mælti:	Bishop said:	The bishop said:
"Veldr þú, Einarr, líftjóni Özurar?"	"Brought-about you, Einar, loss-of-life Ossur?"	"Did you bring about Ossur's loss of life, Einar?"
Hann svarar:	He answered:	He answered:
"Því veld ek víst".	"Because willed I certainly".	"This I willed certainly".
Byskup mælti:	The-bishop said:	The bishop said:
"Eigi eru slík verk góð, en þó er várkunn á".	"Not are-they such work good, but though is pity about".	"Such work is not good, but there is pity about it".
Brandr bað, at þvá skyldi líkinu ok syngja yfir.	Brand bid, that washed should the-body and sung over.	Brand asked that the body should be washed and a service sung over.
Byskup kvað mundu gefa tóm til þess.	Bishop said would give time to this.	The bishop said that there would be time to give to this,
Ok sátu menn undir borðum ok fóru at öllu tómliga, ok fekk byskup svá fremi menn til at syngja yfir líkinu, er Einarr bað þess ok kvað þat sama at gera þat með sæmð.	And sat people under the-tables and went to all time-like, and went bishop so provided men to that sing over the-body, as Einar bid this and said that same that to-do that with honour.	and the people sat at the tables taking their time, and so it went that the bishop provided men to sing over the body as Einar had asked, saying that it should be done with some honour.
Byskup kvaðst ætla, at þat mun réttara at grafa hann eigi at kirkju, "en þó við bæn þína skal hann hér jarða at þessi kirkju, at eigi er heimilisprestr".	The-bishop said supposed, to that would more-correct to grave him not at church, "but though with bidding yours shall he here earthed to this church, that not with local-priest".	The bishop supposed that it would be more correct not to bury him at a church "but because of your asking, he shall be buried at this church that does not have a resident priest".
Ok fekk hann eigi til fyrr kennimenn yfir at syngja en áðr var um lík búit.	And got he not to for priests over to sing but after was about the-body prepared.	And he did not get priests to sing over him as his body was being prepared.
Þá mælti Einarr:	Then said Einar:	Then Einar said:

The Tale of the Greenlanders (II) (The Tale of Einarr Sokkason) (Old Norse)

Old Norse	Literal	English
"Nú hafa orðit í stökki brögð ok ekki lítt af yðru tilstilli, en hér eiga þó hlut í ofsamenn miklir, ok get ek, at stórir úfar rísi á með oss".	"Now has-been become in blood-splattered chest and not little of your agency, but here not though part in overbearing-men much, and get I, that badly misfortune giants of with us".	"Now there has become bloodshed, in no small amount by your doing, and here are very powerful men, and I can tell that a great misfortune will be with us".
Byskup kvaðst vænta, at menn munu þessum ofsa af sér hrinda, en unna sæmðar fyrir mál þetta ok umdæmis, ef eigi væri með ofsa at gengit.	The-bishop said hoped, that people would this violence of themselves repel, but win honour for matter this and area, if not was with violence of going.	The bishop said that he hoped that the people who would bring this violence would be repelled, and that they would win honour in this matter as long as there was no violence.

5

Old Norse	Literal	English
Tíðendi þessi spurðust, ok fréttu þat kaupmenn.	News this heard-of, and found-out the trading-men.	News of this was heard of, and it was found out among the merchants.
Þá mælti Ketill Kálfsson:	Then said Ketil Son-of-Kalf:	Then Ketil Kalfsson said:
"Ekki fór fjarri getu minni, at honum mundi höfuðgjarnt verða".	"Not for far ability mine, that he would headstrong be".	"It is not outside of my ability if he would be headstrong".
Maðr hét Símon, frændi Özurar, mikill maðr ok sterkr.	Man was-named Simon, kinsman Ossur, great man and strong.	There was a man named Simon, a kinsman of Ossur, a great and strong man.
Ketill kvað vera mega, ef Símon fylgði atgervi sinni, at hann mun muna dráp Özurar, frænda síns.	Ketil said to-be may, of Simon follow plan his, that he would remember killing Of-Ossur, kinsman his.	Ketil said that if Simon followed his plan "that he would remember the killing of his kinsman Ossur".
Símon kvaðst þar eigi mundu ferlig orð um hafa.	Simon said that not would-be fair words about had.	Simon said that there would be no good words to be had about it.
Ketill lét búa skip þeira ok sendi menn á fund Kolbeins stýrimanns ok sagði honum tíðendin, "ok segið honum svá, at ek skal fara með máli á hendr Einari, því at mér eru kunnig grænlenzk lög, ok er ek búinn til við þá.	Ketil had prepared ship theirs and sent men to meet Kolbein steersman and said to-him the-news, "and say to-him so, that I shall travel with the-matter in hand Einar, because that to-me they-are known Greenlandic laws, and that I prepared to with them.	Ketil had prepared their ship and sent men to meet Kolbein the steersman and tell him the news "and say to him that I will prosecute Einar for the matter in hand, because the Greenlandic laws are known to me, and I am prepared to deal with them.

The Tale of the Greenlanders (II) (The Tale of Einarr Sokkason) (Old Norse)

Old Norse	Literal	English
Höfum vér ok mikinn liðskost, ef at oss kemst".	Have we-are and much force, of to us come".	We have a great advantage of company if it comes to us".
Símon kvaðst vilja Ketils ráðum fram fara.	Simon said wished-for Ketil's advice from going.	Simon said that he wished for Ketil's advice going forward.
Síðan fór hann ok hitti Kolbein, sagði honum vígit ok þar með orðsending Ketils ok þeir skyldu snúast til liðveizlu við þá ór Vestribyggð ok sækja til þings þeira Grænlendinga.	Then went he and found Kolbein, said to-him killing and there with word-sending Ketil's and they should return to support with then out-of Vestribyggd and seek to assembly theirs Greenland.	Then he went and found Kolbein, and told him of the killing, and that they should return to support them at Vestribyggd and attend the Greenland assembly.
Kolbeinn kvaðst koma mundu at vissu, ef hann mætti, ok kvaðst vilja, at Grænlendingum yrði þat eigi hagkeypi at drepa menn þeira.	Kolbein said come would to know, if he might, and said willed, to Greenland become that not good-bargain that killing men theirs.	Kolbein said that they would certainly come if he did and said that he wanted the Greenlanders to not have to kill their men.
Ketill tók þegar mál af Símoni ok fór með nökkura sveit manna, en sagði, at þeir kaupmenn skyldu halda skjótt eftir, "ok hafið varning með yðr".	Ketil took them the-matter of Simon and went with some company men, but said, that they trading-men should rather away afterwards, "and have wares with you".	Ketil immediately took the matter with Simon and went with a few men, but said that the merchants should leave quickly "and take your goods with you".
Kolbeinn fór þegar, er honum kómu þessi orð, bað ok félaga sína fara til þings ok kveðst þá hafa svá mikla sveit, at óvíst væri, at Grænlendingar sætu yfir hlut þeira.	Kolbein went straightaway, when he came these words, asked and companions his went to the-assembly and said then had so much company, that uncertain was, that Greenlanders reconcile over lot theirs.	Kolbein left as soon as these words came to him, and asked his companions to go to the assembly and declared that they had such a large force that it was uncertain that the Greenlanders would be able to handle their lot.
Nú hittust þeir Kolbeinn ok Ketill ok báru ráð sín saman.	Now found they Kolbein and Ketil and carried advice theirs together.	Now they met Kolbein and Ketil and discussed their advice.
Hvárrtveggi þeira var gildr maðr.	Each of-them was valid man.	Each of them was a valid man.
Nú fóru þeir, ok bægði þeim veðr, ok komast þó fram ok höfðu mikla sveit manna, en þó minni en þeir hugðu.	Now travelled they, and prevented them weather, and came though from and they-had large company of-men, but though less than they thought.	Now they travelled and the weather prevented them but they came through it, and they had a large company of men but less than they thought.

The Tale of the Greenlanders (II) (The Tale of Einarr Sokkason) (Old Norse)

Old Norse	Literal	English
Nú kómu menn til þings.	Now came men to the-assembly.	Now the men came to the assembly.
Sokki var þar kominn Þórisson.	Sokki was there coming Son-of-Thorri.	Sokki Thorisson came there too.
Hann var vitr maðr ok var þá gamall ok mjök tekinn til at gera um mál manna.	He was wise man and was then old and very taken to that doing about matters peoples'.	He was a wise man and was very old by then, and was often taken to dealing with peoples' matters.
Hann gengr á fund þeira Kolbeins ok Ketils ok kvaðst vilja leita um sættir.	He went to meet them Kolbein and Ketil and said willed seek about reconciliation.	He went to meet Kolbein and Ketil and said that he wished to seek reconciliation.
"Vil ek bjóðast til",	"Will I offer to",	"I wish to offer",
segir hann, "at gera í milli yðvar,	said he, "to make in between you,	he said, "to make this between you.
ok þótt mér sé meiri vandi á við Einar, son minn, þá skal þat þó um gera, er mér ok öðrum vitrum mönnum lízt nær sanni".	and though I him more custom to with Einar, son mine, then shall it though about be-done, that I and others wise men behold nearer the-truth".	And even though I have a bigger custom with Einar my son, it will still be about what I and other wise men think is closer to the truth".
Ketill kvaðst ætla, at þeir mundi málum fram halda til málsfyllingar, en fyrirkveðast eigi at taka sættir, "en þó er ört at gengit við oss, en höfum ekki vanizt því hér til at minnka várn hlut".	Ketil said intended, that they would the-matter from hold until the-matter-fulfilling, but refusing not to take reconciliation, "but though we-are swiftly to going with us, but have not custom as here to of decreased our lot".	Ketil said that they intended to take the matter to its conclusion, and refused to rule out a reconciliation "and though we are being treated swiftly, we are not accustomed to reducing our share".
Sokki kveðst ætla, at þeir munu eigi jafnt at vígi standa, ok kvað óvíst, at þeir fengi meiri sæmð, þó hann dæmði eigi.	Sokki said supposed, that they would not equal to battle stand, and said uncertain, that they would-get more honour, though he judged not.	Sokki said he supposed that they won't be equal if it came to a battle, and said it was uncertain that they would get any more honour though he would not judge the matter.
Kaupmenn gengu at dómi, ok hafði Ketill mál frammi á hönd Einari.	The-merchants went to court, and had Ketil the-case from in hand Einar.	The merchants went to court and Ketil had the case in hand from Einar.
Þat mælti Einarr:	This said Einar:	Then Einar said:
"Þat mun víða spyrjast, ef þeir bera oss hér málum"	"It will-be widely known-about, if they bear us here cases	"It will be widely known about if they bear this case here"

The Tale of the Greenlanders (II) (The Tale of Einarr Sokkason) (Old Norse)

Old Norse	Literal	English
ok gekk at dóminum ok hleypir upp, ok fengu þeir ekki haldit.	and went to the-court and released up, and got they not holding.	and went into the court and broke it up and they did not get their proceedings.
Þá mælti Sokki:	Then said Sokki:	Then Sokki said:
"Kostr skal enn þess, er ek bauð, at sættast ok gera ek um málit".	"Choice shall one this, that I asked-for, to reconcile and make I about the-case".	"The choice shall be one that I asked for to reconcile, and I shall make the case".
Ketill kveðst ætla, at þat mundi nú ekki verða, "er þú leggr til yfirbóta, þat er þó er inn sami ójafnaðr Einars um þetta mál",	Ketil said intended, that it would now not be, "but you propose to over-compensation, it that though is the same unequal Einar about that case",	Ketil said that he supposed that it would now not be "but to propose more compensation would be just as unequal to Einar in the case"
ok skilðu at því.	and separated to accordingly.	and they separated accordingly.
En því kómu kaupmenn eigi ór Vestribyggð til þings, at þá var andviðri, er þeir váru búnir með tveim skipum.	But then came the-merchants alone from Vestribyggd to the-assembly, that then were the-storm, that they were prepared with two ships.	But then came the merchants from Vestribyggd to the assembly that were in the storm and prepared with two ships.
En at miðju sumri skyldi sætt gera á Eiði.	But in the-middle of-summer should settled be in Eid.	But in the middle of summer a settlement should be made at Eid.
Þá kómu þeir kaupmenn vestan ok lögðu at við nes nökkut, ok hittust þeir þá allir saman ok áttu stefnur.	Then came they the-trading-men western and laid at with headland some, and met they then all together and had plans.	Then the merchants came from the west and laid at a certain headland, and they all met up and made their plans.
Þá mælti Kolbeinn, at eigi skyldi svá nær hafa gengit um sættirnar, ef þeir hefði allir samt verit, "en þat þykkir mér nú ráð, at vér farim allir til þessa fundar með slíkum föngum sem til eru".	Then said Kolbein, that not should so close have been about reconciliation, if they had all together been, "but it seems to-me now advisable, that we go all to this meeting with such resources as to they-are".	Then Kolbein said that it should not have been so close to a reconciliation if they had all been together "but it seems to me now advisable that we all go to this meeting with such resources as they are".
Ok svá var, at þeir fóru ok leyndust í leynivági einum skammt frá byskupsstólnum.	And so was, it they went and innermost in hidden-creek one a-short-distance from the-bishop's-seat.	And so it was that they went to the innermost of a certain hidden creek a short distance from the bishop's seat.

The Tale of the Greenlanders (II) (The Tale of Einarr Sokkason) (Old Norse)

Old Norse	Literal	English
Þat bar saman at byskupsstólinum, at hringði til hámessu, ok þat at Einarr Sokkason kom.	It bore together that the-bishop's-seat, that called to high-mass, and it that Einar Son-of-Sokki came.	And so it came together that the bishop's seat called a high mass, and Einar Sokkason arrived.
Ok er kaupmennirnir heyrðu þetta, þá sögðu þeir, at mikla skyldi gera virðing til Einars, at hringja skal í mót honum, ok kváðu slík mikil endemi ok urðu illa við.	And when the-trading-men heard that, then said they, that great should be-done worthiness to Einar, to call shall in meeting him, and saying such great unheard-of and became angry with.	And when the merchants heard that they said that it was paying a great honour to Einar to meet him in such a way, saying that it was a great unheard of, and they became angry with.
Kolbeinn mælti:	Kolbein said:	Kolbein said:
"Verðið eigi illa við þetta, því at svá mætti at berast, at þetta yrði at líkhringingu, áðr kveld kæmi".	"Become not ill with this, because that so might that bear, that this would to funeral-procession, before night comes".	"Do not become ill with this, because it might come to be that this will be a funeral procession before night comes".
Nú kómu þeir Einarr ok settust niðr í brekku einni.	Now came they Einar and sat down in the-slope alone.	Now came Einar and his men and sat down alone.
Sokki lét fram gripi til virðingar ok þá, er til gjalds váru ætlaðir.	Sokki laid-out from treasure to worthiness and then, when the payment was intended.	Sokki laid out treasures of value that were intended for payment.
Ketill mælti:	Ketil said:	Ketil said:
"Þat vil ek, at vit Hermundr Koðránsson virðim gripina".	"That will I, that with Hermund Son-of-Kodran worthiness treasure".	"I wish for Hermund Kodransson and I to value these treasures".
Sokki kvað svá vera skyldu.	Sokki said so being would.	Sokki said that it would be so.
Símon, frændi Özurar, sýndi á sér ópekkðarsvip ok reikaði hjá, meðan gripagjaldit var sett.	Simon, kinsman Of-Ossur, showed of himself dishonourable and wandered by, while the-artefact-fee was set.	Simon, a kinsman of Ossur, showed himself to be dishonourable and wandered by while the artefacts were being set.
Síðan var fram borin spangabrynja ein forn.	Then was from brought plate-mail one of-old.	Then an ancient plate mal was brought out.
Símon mælti þá:	Simon said then:	Then Simon said:
"Svívirðliga er slíkt boðit fyrir slíkan mann sem Özurr var",	"Disgracefully is such offering for such man as Ossur was",	"Such an offering is disgraceful for such a man as Ossur was"

The Tale of the Greenlanders (II) (The Tale of Einarr Sokkason) (Old Norse)

Old Norse	Literal	English
ok kastaði brynjunni á völlinn á burt ok gekk upp at þeim, er þeir sátu í brekkunni.	and cast the-armour on the-field and way and went up to them, as they sat on the-slope.	and he threw the armour away on the field and went up to them as they sat on the slope.
Ok er þat sá þeir Grænlendingar, þá spretta þeir upp ok horfðu forbrekkis ok í móti honum Símoni.	And when that saw they Greenlanders, then sprang they up and looked downhill and in facing him Simon.	And when the Greenlanders saw that, they sprang up and looked downhill at Simon and faced towards him.
Ok því næst gekk Kolbeinn upp hjá þeim, er þeir horfðu allir frá, ok slæst á bak þeim ok fór einn frá sínum mönnum,	And then next went Kolbein up beside them, when they looked all away-from, and slipped in back of-them and went alone from his men,	And then Kolbein went up beside them whey they all looked away and slipped behind them alone from his men.
ok var þat jafnsnemma, at hann komst á bak Einari ok hjó með öxi milli herða honum ok Einars öx kom í höfuð Símoni, ok fengu báðir banasár.	and was it equally-early, that he came to back Einar and struck with an-axe between shoulders his and Einar's axe came in head Simon's, and got both death-wounds.	And it was just as soon that he got behind Einar and cut him with an axe between his shoulders, and Einar's axe hit Simon in the head and both received mortal wounds.
Einarr mælti, er hann fell:	Einar said, when he fell:	Einar said when he fell:
"Slíks var at ván".	"Such was it expected".	"It was so as I expected".
Síðan hljóp Þórðr, fóstbróðir Einars, at Kolbeini ok vildi höggva hann, en Kolbeinn snaraðist við honum ok stakk fram öxarhyrnunni ok kom í barkann Þórði, ok hafði hann þegar bana.	Then ran Thord, foster-brother Einar's, to Kolbein and wanted to-strike him, but Kolbein caught-up with him and thrust from axe-horn and came in throat Thord's, and had he instantly killed.	Then Thord, Einar's foster brother, ran to Kolbein and wanted to cut him down, but Kolbein caught up with him and stuck out the axe horn and hit Thord in the throat, killing him instantly.
Síðan slær í bardaga með þeim.	Then struck to battle with them.	Then a battle was struck between them.
Byskup sat hjá Einari, ok andaðist hann í knjám honum.	Bishop sat beside Einar, and died he in knees his.	The bishop sat beside Einar and he died in his lap.
Steingrímr hét maðr, er þat mælti, at þeir skyldi gera svá vel at berjast eigi, ok gekk á milli með nökkura menn, en hvárirtveggja váru svá óðir, at Steingrímr var lagðr sverði í gegnum í þessi hríð.	Steingrim was-named a-man, who this said, that they should do so well to fight not, and went in between with some men, but either-side were so angry, that Steingrim was laid to-the-sword in through in this time.	There was a man named Steingrim who said that they would do well not to fight and went in between some of the men, but either side was so angry that Steingrim was laid to the sword through him in this time.

The Tale of the Greenlanders (II) (The Tale of Einarr Sokkason) (Old Norse)

Old Norse	Literal	English
Einarr andaðist uppi á brekkunni við búð Grænlendinga.	Einar died up on the-slope by booth The-Greenlanders'.	Einar died up on the slope by the Greenlanders' booth.
Ok nú urðu menn sárir mjök, ok kómust þeir Kolbeinn til skips með þrjá sína menn vegna ok fóru síðan yfir Einarsfjörð til Skjálgsbúða.	And now became men wounded much, and came they Kolbein to ships with three their men slain and went then over Einarsfjord to Skjalgsbud.	And now men became much wounded and Kolbein and his men came to their ships with three men killed and went over to Einarsfjord to Skjalgsbud.
Þar váru kaupskipin ok váru þá mjök í búnaði.	There were merchant-ships and were then much in preparations.	The merchant ships were there and they were very much prepared.
Kolbeinn kvað í hafa gerzt nökkura róstu, "ok vil ek ætla, at Grænlendingar uni nú ekki betr við en áðr".	Kolbein said that had done some uproar, "and will I suppose, that Greenlanders like now not better with than before".	Kolbein said that there had been some uproar "and I would like to say that the Greenlanders are now no better pleased than before".
Ketill mælti:	Ketil said:	Ketil said:
"Sannyrði gafst þér, Kolbeinn",	"True-words gave to-you, Kolbein",	"You gave true words Kolbein",
sagði hann, "at vér myndim heyra líkhringingina, áðr vér færim í brott, ok ætla ek, at hann Einarr sé dauðr borinn til kirkju".	said he, "that we would hear the-funeral-procession, before we travel to away, and suppose I, that he Einar is dead carried to the-church".	he said, "that we would hear the funeral procession before we travel away and I suppose that Einar who is dead will be carried to the church".
Kolbeinn kveðst heldr þannig hafa at stutt.	Kolbein said rather that-way had it supported.	Kolbein said that it was rather that way, that he had supported it.
Ketill mælti:	Ketil said:	Ketil said:
"Þess er ván, at Grænlendingar muni sækja á várn fund, ok kalla ek ráð, at menn haldi á búnaði sínum eftir föngum ok sé allir á skipum um nætr".	"This is expect, that The-Greenlanders will seek to ours meet, and call I advice, that men hold of equipment theirs after resources and are all to ships about night".	"It is expected that the Greenlanders will seek to meet us, and I advise that the men take hold of their equipment and resources and all stay on the ships overnight".
Ok svá gerðu þeir.	And so did they.	And so they did.

The Tale of the Greenlanders (II) (The Tale of Einarr Sokkason) (Old Norse)

Old Norse	Literal	English
Sokki harmaði mjök þessi tíðendi ok bað menn fulltingis at veita sér vígsgengi.	Sokki harmed much this news and asked men assistance to grant him in-battle.	Sokki was much harmed by this news and asked the men to grant him assistance in battle.

6

Old Norse	Literal	English
Hallr hét maðr.	Hall was-named man.	There was a man named Hall.
Hann bjó at Sólarfjöllum, vitr maðr ok góðr bóndi.	He lived at Solarfjoll, wise man and good farmer.	He lived at Solarfjoll, he was a wise man and a good farmer.
Hann var í liði með Sokka ok kom síðast með sínu liði.	He was in company with Sokki and came last with his team.	He was in company with Sokki and was the last to come to his team.
Hann mælti til Sokka:	He said to Sokki:	He said to Sokki:
"Ekki vænlig lízt mér þín ætlan, at leggja smáskipum at stórskipum við slíkan viðbúnað sem ek hygg, at þeir muni hafa,	"Not hopeful behold I your intention, to lay small-ships to large-ships with such preparation as I think, that they shall have,	"I am not hopeful of your intention to lay small ships against large ships with such preparations as I think they will have.
en ek veit eigi, hversu traust lið er þú hefir, en allir vaskir menn munu vel gefast, en hinir munu hlífast meir, ok verða höfuðsmenn fyrir þat uppgefnir, ok horfir þá enn þungligar várr málahlutr en áðr.	but I know not, how-so trust team is you have, but all brave men should well give, but others should protect more, and become head-men for that up-given, and where then but the-more-difficult our matter-lot than before.	But I don't know how strong a team you have, but all the good men will give well, but the others will be more careful, and the leaders will be exhausted because of it, and then our affairs will be even more difficult than before.
Nú sýnist mér ráð, ef menn skulu at leggja, at eiðar fari fram, at hverr maðr skyli annathvárt hér falla eða hafa sigr".	Now seems to-me advisable, if men shall to allow, that oath go from, to each man shall other-either here fall or have victory".	Now it seems to me that if men are to make an oath, each man shall either fall here or be victorious".
En við þessi orð Halls dignuðu menn mjök.	But with this word Hall's pride lessened much.	But at this word of Hall's, peoples' pride lessened much.
Sokki mælti:	Sokki said:	Sokki said:
"Eigi munum vér þó skilja við þetta, at ósett sé málunum".	"Not shall we though part with this, that unsettled is the-matter".	"However, we will not part with this, that things are not settled".

The Tale of the Greenlanders (II) (The Tale of Einarr Sokkason) (Old Norse)

Old Norse	Literal	English
Hallr kvaðst mundu leita um sættir milli þeira ok kallaði á kaupmenn ok mælti:	Hall said should seek about reconciliation between them and called the trading-men and spoke:	Hall said that they should seek reconciliation between them and called the merchants and spoke:
"Hvárt skal mér fritt at ganga á fund yðvarn?"	"Whether shall I peace to go to meet with-you?"	"Should I be at peace to go to a meeting with you?"
Þeir Kolbeinn ok Ketill svara, at honum skyldi fritt.	They Kolbein and Ketil answered, that to-him should-be peace.	Kolbein and his men answered that he should be at peace.
Síðan hitti hann þá ok lét nauðsyn, at málum væri sett eftir slík stórvirki.	Then met he then and had necessary, to matter should-be settled after such great-works.	Then he met them and made it necessary that matters should be settled after such great deeds.
Þeir kváðust nú búnir við hváru, sem aðrir vildi, kváðu af þeim landsmönnum allan þennan ójafnað staðit hafa, "en nú, er þú sýnir svá mikla góðgirnd, þá unum vér því, at þú gerir í milli vár".	They said now prepared with each, as other willed, saying of them lands-men all then unequal stood have, "but now, are you showed so much good-will, then among us therefore, that you make to between us".	They said they were ready to do whatever others wanted, they said of those countrymen who have been through this uneven situation "but now you are showing so much kindness, we hope that you do among us".
Hann kvaðst eftir því gera mundu ok dæma, er honum sýndist réttligast, hversu sem hvárum líkaði.	He said after therefore be-done should and deemed, that to-him seemed correctness, how-so as each liked.	He said that he would do what he thought was the right thing to do, however everyone liked it.
Síðan var þetta fyrir Sokka borit.	Then was that for Sokki borne.	Then this was put before Sokki.
Hann kveðst ok mundu una umdæmi Halls.	He said and would content about-judgement Hall's.	He said that he would be content with Hall's judgement about it.
Kaupmenn skyldu um nætr at búnaði sínum vera ok kváðu Sokka ekki annat líka en þeir yrði í brottu sem fyrst, "en ef þeir seinka búnað sinn ok gera mér skapraun í því, þá er vís ván, at þeir skulu bótalausir, ef þeir verða teknir".	The-trading-men should about the-night to equipment theirs be and said Sokki not other like but they be to away as first, "but if they delay preparations theirs and make to-me temperament in because, then be aware hope, that they shall boat-lose, if they become taken".	The merchants had to make their preparations through the night and Sokki said that there was no other way except that they were to be away as soon as possible "but if they delay in their preparations and make to my temperament, then they shall lose their boat if they become taken".

The Tale of the Greenlanders (II) (The Tale of Einarr Sokkason) (Old Norse)

Old Norse	Literal	English
Nú skilðu þeir at því, ok var á sáttarfund kveðit.	Now separated they that accordingly, and were in peace-meeting declared.	Now they separated accordingly and a reconciliation meeting was declared.
Ketill mælti:	Ketil said:	Ketil said:
"Ekki horfir skjótliga búnaðr várr, en vistaföng þverra heldr, ok er þat mitt ráð at leita eftir vistunum, ok veit ek, hvar sá maðr býr, er mikinn mat á, ok kalla ek ráð at sækja eftir".	"Not looks shortly equipment ours, but resources running-out rather, and is it my advice to seek after provisions, and know I, where so man prepared, is much food to, and call I advice to seek after".	"It does not look like our equipment will be prepared shortly, and resources are running out, and it is my advice to seek provisions, and I know where there is a man who has much food, and I advise we seek him out".
Þeir kváðust þess albúnir.	They said this all-prepared.	They said they were all ready.
Síðan hlupu þeir upp eina nátt frá skipum, þrír tigir manna saman, allir vápnaðir, ok kómu at bænum, ok var þar autt allt.	Then ran they up one night from the-ship, three tens of-men together, all weaponed, and came to dwelling, and were there empty all.	They hurried up one night from the ship, and thirty men together, all armed, came to the dwelling but it was all empty.
Þórarinn hét bóndi sá, er þar bjó.	Thorarin was-named a-farmer that, was there settled.	Thorarin was the name of the farmer that was settled there.
Ketill mælti:	Ketil said:	Ketil said:
"Eigi hefir mitt ráð vel gefizt",	"Not has my advice well given",	"My advice has not given well"
ok fara síðan í brott frá bænum ok ofan á leið til skipa, ok var þar hrísótt, er þeir fóru.	and went then to away from the-dwelling and over to the-way to the-ships, and were there shrubs, where they went.	and then went away from the dwelling and over to the ships, and there were shrubs along where they went.
Þá mælti Ketill:	Then said Ketil:	Then Ketil said:
"Syfjar mik",	"Sleepy me",	"I feel sleepy",
sagði hann, "ok verð ek at sofa".	said he, "and deserve I to sleep".	he said, "and I deserve to sleep".
Þeir kváðu þat ekki mjök ráðligt.	They said that not much advisable.	They said that it was not advisable,
En þó lagðist hann niðr ok sofnaði, en þeir sátu yfir.	But though laid he down and slept, while they sat over.	but he laid down and slept while they sat and watched over.

The Tale of the Greenlanders (II) (The Tale of Einarr Sokkason) (Old Norse)

Old Norse	Literal	English
Litlu síðar vaknaði hann ok mælti:	Little later awoke he and said:	A little later he awoke and said:
"Margt hefir fyrir mik borit.	"Many have before me brought.	"Much has brought before me.
Hvat mun varða, þótt vér kippim upp hríslu þessi, er hér er undir höfði mér?"	What should happen, though we jerk up clump this, that here is under head mine?"	What would happen if we jerked up this clump that is here under my head?"
Þeir kippðu upp hríslunni, ok var þar undir jarðhús mikit.	They pulled up the-branch, and was there under earth-house great.	They pulled up the branches and under it was a great cave.
Ketill mælti:	Ketil said:	Ketil said:
"Vitum fyrst, hvat hér er fanga".	"Know-we first, what here is provisions".	"We should know first what provisions are here".
Þeir fundu þar sex tigi slátrgripa ok tólf vættir smjörs, skreið mikla.	They found there six tens carcasses and twelve weights of-butter, fish much.	They found sixty carcasses, twelve weights of butter, and a lot of fish.
"Vel er þat",	"Well is that",	"That is good",
sagði Ketill, "at ek hefi eigi villt upp borit fyrir yðr".	said Ketil, "that I have not wildly up presented for you".	said Ketil, "that I have not wildly brought up for you".
Nú fara þeir til skips með feng sinn.	Now went they to the-ships with provisions theirs.	Now they went to the ships with their provisions.
Nú líðr at sáttarfundinum, ok kómu hvárirtveggju til þess fundar, kaupmenn ok landsmenn.	Now passed to reconciliation-meeting, and came either-side to this meeting, trading-men and lands-men.	Now it passed to the reconciliation meeting, and both sides came to the meeting, the merchants and the landsmen.
Þá mælti Hallr:	Then said Hall:	Then Hall said:
"Sú er sáttargerð mín yðvar í milli, at ek vil, at á standist víg Özurar ok Einars, en fyrir manna mun skulu koma sekðir Austmanna, at þeir skulu hér ekki eiga vist né væri.	"So is settlement mine yours in between, that I will, to a to-stand slaying Ossur and Einar, but for men less would come penalty Eastern-men, that they shall here not own resources nor should-they.	"This is my settlement among you, that I wish for the killing of Ossur to stand for that of Einar, but for the loss of men, the Norwegians shall not be here nor shall they own resources here.

The Tale of the Greenlanders (II) (The Tale of Einarr Sokkason) (Old Norse)

Old Norse	Literal	English
Þau víg skulu ok jöfn vera, Steingríms bónda ok Símonar, Kráks Austmanns ok Þorfinns Grænlendings, Víghvats Austmanns ok Bjarna Grænlendings, Þóris ok Þórðar.	Those killings shall and even be, Steingrim's farmer and Simon, Krak The-Easterner and Thorfin The-Greenlander, Vighvats The-Easterner and Bjarn The-Greenlander, Thori and Thord.	Those killings shall be even, Steingrim the farmer and Simon, Krak the Easterner and Thorfin the Greenlander, Vighvats the Easterner and Bjarn the Greenlander, Thori and Thord.
Nú er einn óbættr várr maðr, er Þóarinn heitir, ómegðarmaðr.	Now that one uncompensated our man, that Thorarin is-named, poor-man.	Now one of our men is uncompensated, named Thorarin, a poor man.
Hann skal fé bæta".	He shall wealth be-compensated".	He shall be compensated with wealth".
Sokki hvat sér þungt gerðir líka ok svá öðrum Grænlendingum, er þannig fór um mannjafnað.	Sokki that himself unhappy made alike and so other Greenlanders, that that-way went about equal-man.	Sokki said that he was unhappy with how it was done that Greenlanders and the other men were equally paired in that way.
Hallr kvaðst ætla, at þar muni þó staðar nema hans ummæli.	Hall said intend, that there should though stand taking his about-matter.	Hall said he intended that it should though stand as he took the matter,
Ok við þat skilðu þeir.	And with that separated they.	and with that they separated.
Síðan rak ís at ok þakði alla fjörðu, ok hugðu Grænlendingar þá gott til, ef þeir mætti taka þá ok þeir færi eigi svá brott sem mælt var.	Then drifted ice to and covered all the-fjord, and thought The-Greenlanders then good to, of they might take then and they travel alone so away as told were.	Then ice drifted in and covered the whole fjord, and the Greenlanders thought it would be good if they could take them and they didn't go away as they were told.
En við þat sjálft at mánaðarmótit kom, þá rak í brott allan ísinn, ok gaf kaupmönnum brott af Grænlandi, ok skilðu við þat.	But with that itself to month's-end came, then drove to way all ice, and gave the-trading-men away of Greenland, and separated with it.	But as soon as the end of the month came, all the ice was swept away and the merchants left Greenland and parted with it.
Þeir kómu við Nóreg.	They came to Norway.	They came to Norway.

The Tale of the Greenlanders (II) (The Tale of Einarr Sokkason) (Old Norse)

Old Norse	Literal	English
Kolbeinn hafði haft einn hvítabjörn af Grænlandi ok fór með dýrit á fund Haralds konungs gilla ok gaf honum ok tjáði fyrir konungi, hversu þungs hlutar Grænlendingar váru af verðir, ok færði þá mjök í róg.	Kolbein had had one white-bear of Greenland and went with the-animal to meet Harald the-king residence and gave him and told for the-kind, how-so heavily lot The-Greenlanders were of being, and brought them much to slander.	Kolbein had had one white bear from Greenland and took the animal to King Harald's meeting and gave it to him and expressed to the king how much of a burden the Greenlanders were becoming and brought them into great slander.
En konungr spurði annat síðar, ok þótti honum Kolbeinn hafa fals fyrir sik borðit, ok kómu engi laun fyrir dýrit.	But the-king learned otherwise later, and thought he Kolbein had a-falsehood for him bore-up, and came no reward for the-animal.	But the king learned otherwise later and it seemed to him that Kolbein had borne up a falsehood for him and there was no reward for the animal.
Síðan hljóp Kolbeinn í flokk með Sigurði slembidjákn ok gekk inn at Haraldi konungi gilla ok veitti honum áverka.	Then ran Kolbein to grouped with Sigurd the-false-deacon and went in to Harald the-king residence and granted to-him a-wound.	Then Kolbein hurried to group with Sigurd the false deacon, and went into King Harald's residence and gave him a wound.
Ok síðan er þeir fóru fyrir Danmörk ok sigldu mjök, en Kolbeinn var á eftirbáti, en veðr hvasst, þá sleit frá bátinn, ok drukknaði Kolbeinn.	And then when they travelled to Denmark and sailed much, but Kolbein was in the-boat-behind, but weather stormy, then tore-up from the-boat, and drowned Kolbein.	And then when they travelled to Denmark their sail was carried much, but Kolbein was in the boat behind in stormy weather which then tore up the boat behind and Kolbein drowned.
En þeir Hermundr kómu til Íslands til ættjarða sinna.	But they The-Hermunds came to Iceland to homelands theirs.	But Hermund and the others came to Iceland, their homeland.
Ok lýkr þar þessi sögu.	And ends here this saga.	And here ends this saga.

Word List *(Old Norse to English)*

Old Norse	English

A, a

aðrir	other
af	from, from, of, of, off
aflat	gain
aftr	back
agir	desirable
albúnir	all-prepared
alla	all
allan	all
allir	all, all
allmjök	all-great
allt	all
allvel	all-well, all-well
andaðist	died, died
andviðri	the-storm
annarra	other
annat	another, another, anything-else, other, otherwise
annathvárt	other-either
Arnald	Arnald (name)
Arnaldr	Arnald (name)
Arnbjarnar	Arnbjarn (name), Arnbjarnar (name)
Arnbjörn	Arnbjorn (name)
at	a, at, by, in, it, of, that, the, to
atburði	events
atgervi	plan
auðit	possible
austmaðr	Eastern-man
austmanna	Eastern-men
austmanns	the-Easterner
austmenn	Eastern-men
autt	empty

Á, á

á	a, about, and, as, at, in, of, on, out, that, the, to
áðr	after, before
áðu	that
árós	river-mouth
átt	had, owned
áttu	had, have
áverka	a-wound

Æ, æ

æðimaðr	of-mind
æpa	shouting
ætla	intend, intended, suppose, supposed
ætlaðir	intended
ætlan	intention
ætluðu	supposed
ætti	had
ættjarða	homelands

B, b

bað	asked, bid
báðir	both
báðu	asked
bæ	a-farm
bæði	asked
bægði	prevented
bæn	bidding, prayers
bænar	prayers
bændr	farmers
bænum	dwelling, the-dwelling
bæta	be-compensated
bak	back
bana	death, killed
banahögg	death-blow
banasár	death-wounds
bar	bore
bardaga	battle
barkann	throat
báru	carried
bátinn	the-boat

Word List (Old Norse to English)

Old Norse	English
bauð	asked-for, invited
beiddi	bid
bein	bones
beinum	bones
bera	bear
berast	bear
berdreyman	clear-dreams
berjast	fight
betr	better
bezt	best
bjarga	rescuing
bjargar	rescue
Bjarna	Bjarn (name)
bjarndýri	a-bear
bjó	lived, prepared, settled
bjóðast	offer
björg	rocks
bjóst	prepared
boðit	offering
bokki	buck
bolöx	the-trunk
bónda	farmer
bóndi	a-farmer, farmer
borð	boards, the-tables
borðit	bore-up, the-table
borðum	the-tables
borin	brought
borinn	carried
borit	borne, brought, presented
bótalausir	boat-lose
Brandr	Brand (name)
Brattahlíð	Brattahlid (place)
bréfum	briefs
brekku	the-slope
brekkunni	the-slope
brenndu	burned
bróðir	brother
brögð	chest
brotit	broken
brott	away, way
brottu	away
brugðit	upset
brynjunni	the-armour
búa	prepared
búð	booth
búinn	prepared
búit	prepared, settled
búnað	preparations
búnaði	equipment, preparations
búnaðr	equipment
búnir	prepared
burt	way
byggðina	the-settlement
býr	prepared
byrrinn	bearing
byskup	a-bishop, bishop, the-bishop
byskupi	the-bishop
byskups	bishop, the-bishop, the-bishop's
byskupsefni	the-bishop-elect
byskupslaust	bishop-less
byskupsstólinum	the-bishop's-seat
byskupsstóll	bishop's-seat
byskupsstólnum	the-bishop's-seat
byskupsstólsins	bishop's-seat
byskupsvígslu	bishop's-appointment

D, d

Old Norse	English
dæma	deemed
dæmði	judged
dag	the-day
Danmarkar	Denmark (place)
Danmörk	Denmark (place)
dauða	dead
dauðr	dead
daun	the-dead
dignuðu	pride
dómi	court, the-court
dóminum	the-court
dómr	judgement
dómrinn	the-judgement
dráp	killing
draum	dream
drauminn	the-dream
drepa	killing
dreymði	dreamed

Word List (Old Norse to English)

Old Norse	English
drukknaði	drowned
duga	aided
dyljast	hiding
dýrit	the-animal

E, e

Old Norse	English
eða	but, or
eðli	nature
ef	if, of
efldr	strengthened
eftir	after, afterwards, followed, following, later, remaining
eftirbáti	the-boat-behind
eftirbátinn	the-after-boat
eið	oath
eiðar	oath
Eiði	Eid (place)
eiðrofa	breach-of-oath
eiga	have, not, own
eigi	alone, no, not
eign	property
eigna	property
eignum	owning
ein	one
eina	one
einangr	alone-going
Einar	Einar (name)
Einari	Einar (name)
Einarr	Einar (name)
Einars	Einar (name), Einar's, Einar's (name)
Einarsfjörð	Einarsfjord (place)
einhverju	one-occasion
einn	a, alone, one
einni	alone
einræði	self-will
einu	one
einum	one
Eiríksfjörð	Eriksfjord (place)
ek	I
ekki	none, not
eldstóar	fire-place
en	and, but, than, while
enda	and
endemi	unheard-of
engi	no, no-one
engum	no
enn	but, one, still
er	and, are, as, be, but, in, is, it, that, the, then, was, we-are, what, when, where, who, with
erendi	errand
erendis	errand
erfitt	difficult
erkibyskup	the-archbishop
erkibyskups	archbishop
eru	are, are-they, they-are, were
eruð	are
Eyjafjöllum	Eyjafjolls (place)

F, f

Old Norse	English
fá	get
færa	bring
færði	brought
færi	going, go-to, travel
færim	travel
fagra	the-fairest
fáliga	coolly
falla	fall
fallinn	fallen, weak
fals	a-falsehood
fang	resources
fanga	provisions
fangit	to-catch
fangs	captivity
fara	going, travel, went, went
fari	go
farim	go
farit	going
fastmæli	opinion
fé	wealth
feðgar	father-and-son
fégjöfum	fee-gifts

Word List (Old Norse to English)

Old Norse	English
féit	wealth
fekk	got, went
fékk	got
félaga	companions
félagar	companions
fell	fell
feng	provisions
fengi	would-get
fengu	got
ferð	journey
ferjuna	the-ferry
ferlig	fair
ferr	went
festa	fix
féván	fee-trust
fimmtán	fifteen
fjár	money
fjárfundinn	wealth-finding
fjarri	far
fjölmenni	following-men, many-people
fjörðinn	fjord
fjörðu	the-fjord
fleiri	more
flokk	grouped
fólk	folk
föngum	resources
fór	for, travelled, went
forbrekkis	downhill
forn	of-old
forsjá	foresight
fóru	travelled, went
fórum	travel, travelled
fóstbróðir	foster-brother
fótum	feet
frá	away-from, from
frænda	kinsman
frændi	kinsman
frændr	kinsman, kinsmen
fram	from
framkvæmð	execution
frammi	from
fremi	provided
fréttu	found-out
fritt	peace
fróði	learned
fulltingis	assistance
fulltingja	fulfil
fulltings	help
fund	meet, meeting
fundar	meet, meeting
fundit	found
fundu	found
fúsari	willing
fylgði	follow, followed
fylgðinni	following
fylgir	followed
fyrir	before, for, foremost, through, to
fyrirgert	before-done
fyrirkveðast	refusing
fyrr	for
fyrst	first, firstly
fýsa	desire

G, g

Old Norse	English
gaf	gave
gafst	gave
gamall	old
ganga	go, going, went
garða	Gardar (place)
gefa	give
gefast	give
gefizt	given
gefnar	given
gegna	pass
gegnt	opposite
gegnum	through
gekk	went
gengit	been, going, walked
gengr	went
gengu	went
gera	be, be-done, do, doing, done, make, to-do, to-give
gerði	did
gerðir	made
gerðist	became
gerðu	did, done, to-do
gerir	make

Word List (Old Norse to English)

Old Norse	English
gersemi	treasure
gert	done, made
gerzt	done
get	get
getu	ability
gildr	valid
gilla	residence
gjalds	payment
góð	good
góða	good
góðan	good
góðgirnd	good-will
góðr	good
göngu	going
Görðum	Gardar (place)
gott	good
grænland	Greenland (place)
Grænlendinga	Greenland (place), Greenlanders (name), the-Greenlanders'
grænlendingar	Greenlanders (name), the-Greenlanders
grænlendings	the-Greenlander
Grænlendingum	Greenland (place), Greenlanders (name)
grænlenzk	Greenlandic (name)
grænlenzkr	a-Greenlander
grænlenzkum	Greenlandic (name)
grafa	grave
grafin	in-the-grave
greiða	assistance
greiðist	paying
greiðslu	compensation
gripagjaldit	the-artefact-fee
gripi	treasure
gripina	treasure
guði	priest
guðs	god's

H, h

Old Norse	English
hægra	right
haf	sea
hafa	had, has, has-been, have
hafði	had
hafi	had
hafið	have
hafskip	sea-going-ship
haft	had, has
hag	circumstances
hagkeypi	good-bargain
hagr	handy
halda	hold, rather, to-hold
haldi	hold
haldit	holding
Hallr	Hall (name)
halls	Hall's, Hall's (name)
hamarrifu	crags
hámessu	high-mass
hann	he, him
hans	him, his, its
haraldi	Harald (name)
haralds	Harald (name)
harmaði	harmed
hásetar	the-crew
haustum	autumn
hefði	had
hefi	have
hefir	has, have
hegna	protected
heim	home
heimamaðr	house-man
heimilisprestr	local-priest
heimta	carry
heimti	presented
heita	be-called
heitir	is-named
heitukötlum	boiling-cauldrons
heldr	rather
heldu	held
héldu	held
hendi	hand
hendr	hand
henta	suitable
hér	here
herða	shoulders
Hermundr	Hermund (name), the-Hermunds (name)
herra	sir
hét	named, was-named

Word List (Old Norse to English)

Old Norse	English
heyra	hear
heyrðu	heard
heyrt	heard
hézt	promised
hingat	here
hinir	others
hitta	find
hitti	found, met
hittust	found, met
hjá	beside, by
hjó	struck
hlaðna	loaded
hlaupa	running
hleypið	discharge
hleypir	released
hleypr	ran
hlífast	protect
hlítt	satisfactory
hljóp	ran
hlupu	ran
hlut	lot, part
hlutar	lot
hlutum	things
hnjóðhamar	hammer
höfðaskip	a-headed-ship
höfðaskipit	head-ship
höfði	head
höfðingja	chieftains
höfðu	had, had-they, they-had
höfuð	head
höfuðgjarnt	headstrong
höfuðsmenn	head-men
höfum	have
höggva	to-strike
höggvit	struck
holdi	flesh
Holtavatnsós	Holtavatnsos (place)
hönd	hand
höndum	handling
honum	he, him, his, to-him
horfðu	looked
horfir	looks, where
hríð	time
hrinda	repel
hringði	called
hringja	call
hríslu	clump
hríslunni	the-branch
hrísótt	shrubs
hugðu	thought
hugi	his-mind
hugr	mind
hún	she
hurðina	the-door
húsa	house
hvar	where
hvárirtveggja	either-side
hvárirtveggju	either-side
hvárrtveggi	each
hvárs	which
hvárt	each, whether
hváru	each
hvárum	each
hvasst	stormy
hvat	that, what
hverfa	turn
hverju	how
hverr	each, who
hversu	how-so
hvítabjörn	white-bear
Hvítserk	Hvitserk (name)
hygg	think

I, i

Old Norse	English
illa	angry, ill
illt	ill
inn	in, the
inni	in
innsiglum	seals
inu	the
it	the, then

Í, í

Old Norse	English
í	about, and, at, in, into, of, on, that, to
ís	ice
Ísa-Steingrímr	Isa-Steingrim (name)

Word List (Old Norse to English)

Old Norse	English
ísinn	ice
íslandi	Iceland (place)
íslands	Iceland (place)

J, j

Old Norse	English
jafnsnemma	equally-early
jafnt	equal
jarða	earthed
jarðhús	earth-house
játtuðu	agreed
jöfn	even
jöklinum	a-glacier
jöklum	glaciers
Jórsalafari	Jerusalem-Traveller (name)

K, k

Old Norse	English
kæmi	comes
Kálfsson	son-of-Kalf (name)
kalla	call, claim
kallaði	called
kallar	called
kambi	comb
kann	can
kastaði	cast
kaupmenn	the-merchants, the-trading-men, trading-men
kaupmennirnir	the-trading-men
kaupmönnum	the-trading-men, trading-men
kaupskip	merchant-ship
kaupskipin	merchant-ships
kaupskipit	merchant-ship
kaupum	a-deal
kemst	come
kennimanns	teaching
kennimenn	priests
kerling	old-woman
kerlingu	the-old-woman
Ketil	Ketil (name)
Ketill	Ketil (name)
Ketils	Ketil (name), Ketil's (name)
Kiðjabergs	Kidjaberg (place)
kilinum	the-keel
kippðu	pulled
kippim	jerk
kirkju	church, the-church
kirkjugarðsins	churchyard
kirkjumessu	church-mass
kirkjuna	the-church
kirkjuvegginn	church-wall
klerkr	cleric
knjám	knees
Koðránsson	son-of-Kodran (name)
Kolbein	Kolbein (name)
Kolbeini	Kolbein (name)
Kolbeinn	Kolbein (name)
Kolbeins	Kolbein (name)
kom	came
koma	come
komast	came, come
kominn	come, coming
komit	come
komst	came
kómu	came
kómust	came
konung	the-king
konungi	the-kind, the-king
konungr	the-king
konungs	the-king, the-king's
konungsbréfum	the-king's-brief
kostr	choice
Kráks	Krak (name)
kunni	known
kunnig	known
kvað	said
kvaðst	said
kváðu	said, saying
kváðust	said
kveðit	declared
kveðja	called
kveðst	said
kveld	night
kyrrlátir	still
kyrrt	still

Word List (Old Norse to English)

Old Norse	English
L, l	
lá	lay
lagðist	laid
lagðr	laid
land	land
Landeyjum	the-Landeys (place)
landi	the-land
landit	the-land
landsins	the-lands
landsmenn	lands-men
landsmönnum	lands-men
Langanes	Langanes (place)
láta	lay-out
laun	reward
legðu	put
leggja	allow, have, lay
leggr	propose
legit	laid
leið	the-way
leit	looked
leita	seek
lengi	long
lengr	longer
lengra	longer
lét	had, laid, laid-out
létu	had
leyndust	innermost
leynivági	hidden-creek
leysti	released
lézt	had
lið	team
liði	company, team
liðit	passed
líðr	passed
liðskost	force
liðu	passed
liðveizlu	support
líftjóni	loss-of-life
lík	the-body
líka	alike, like
líkaði	liked
líkar	like, likes
líkast	likely
líkendi	alike
líkhringingina	the-funeral-procession
líkhringingu	funeral-procession
líkinu	the-body
líkligast	likely
líkum	bodies
lítil	little
lítillæti	humility
lítit	little
litlu	little
lítt	little
lízt	behold
lög	law, laws
lögðu	laid
lögum	law
Lundi	Lund (place)
lýkr	ends
M, m	
maðr	a-man, man
mæla	badly
mælt	told
mælti	said, spoke
mæltu	said
mætti	might
mættir	might
makligast	most
mal	the-matter
mál	a-case, case, matter, matters, the-case, the-matter
málahlutr	matter-lot
máli	discuss, the-matter
málit	the-case
málsfyllingar	the-matter-fulfilling
málum	case, matter, the-matter
málum"	cases
málunum	the-matter
mánaðarmótit	month's-end
mann	a-man, man, the-man
manna	man's, men, of-men, peoples'
manndómsleysi	meanness

Word List (Old Norse to English)

Old Norse	English
mannhættu	dangerous
manni	man
manninum	this-man
mannjafnað	equal-man
mannshræ	dead-body, human-body
mannvænlegr	a-friendly
margt	many
mat	food
mátti	might
með	with
meðallagi	moderately
meðan	as-long-as, while
mega	may
megin	sides
megri	meagre
mein	disease, harm
meir	more
meira	more
meiri	more
menn	lessened, men, people
mér	I, me, mine, to-me
messu	mass
mest	most
mestr	the-most
metnir	important
metorð	esteem
miðju	the-middle
mik	me
mikil	great, much
mikill	great, much
mikils	much
mikinn	much
mikit	a-great, great, many, much
mikla	great, large, much
miklir	much
miklu	much
milli	between
mín	mine
minn	mine
minni	less, mine
minnka	decreased
mínum	mine, my
misst	lost
mitt	my
mjök	much, very
mönnum	men, the-men
morgininn	morning
mót	meet, meeting
móti	facing
mun	less, should, will, will-be, would
muna	remember
mundi	would
mundu	should, would, would-be
muni	shall, should, will, would
munni	mouth
munt	would
muntu	shall-you
munu	may, should, would
munum	shall
myndim	would

N, n

Old Norse	English
náðu	reached
næði	get
nær	as-far, close, nearer
næst	next
nætr	night, the-night
náir	getting
nátt	night
nauðsyn	necessary, needs
né	nor
neðan	below
nema	taking
nenna	bothered
nes	headland
niðr	down
Njálsson	son-of-Njal (name)
nökkur	some
nökkura	some
nökkurar	some
nökkurn	some
nökkurra	something
nökkuru	some
nökkurum	some

Word List (Old Norse to English)

Old Norse	English
nökkut	some
Nóreg	Norway (place)
nóregi	Norway (place)
Nóregs	Norway (place)
norrænir	Nordic (name)
norrænn	Nordic (name)
nótt	the-night
nú	not, now
nytjum	use

O, o

Old Norse	English
Odda	Odda (place)
of	of
ofan	above, over
ofsa	violence
ofsamenn	overbearing-men
oft	often
ok	also, and
orð	a-word, word, words
orða	words
orðinn	the-words
orðit	become, have-become
orðsending	word-sending
oss	to-us, us

Ó, ó

Old Norse	English
óbættr	uncompensated
óbyggðir	un-settled
óbyggðum	the-unsettled-land
óðir	angry
óforsjáll	impulsive
ófúss	reluctant
ójafnað	un-equal
ójafnaðr	unequal
ómegðarmaðr	poor-man
ór	from, out-from, out-of
órræði	solution
órræðit	solution
ósæmð	dishonourable
ósett	unsettled
óþekkðarsvip	dishonourable, ungraceful
óvirðing	un-worthy
óvíst	uncertain

Ö, ö

Old Norse	English
öðru	another, other
öðrum	other, others
öllu	all
öllum	all, ill
ört	swiftly
öx	axe
öxarhyrnunni	axe-horn
öxi	an-axe, axe
Özur	Ossur (name)
Özurar	of-Ossur (name), Ossur (name)
Özuri	Ossur (name)
Özurr	Ossur (name)

R, r

Old Norse	English
ráð	advice, advisable, decide
ráða	advice
ráðast	arrange, be-arranged
ráðist	advise
ráðligt	advisable
ráðum	advice
rak	drifted, drove
raunar	actually
réð	commanded
réðist	deal
réðst	ruled
refsa	punish
reið	rode
reiðisvipr	angry
reiðr	angry
reikaði	wandered
rétt	rights
réttara	more-correct
réttligast	correctness
reyndust	gave-him

Word List (Old Norse to English)

Old Norse	English
rísi	giants
rjúfa	break-open
róg	slander
róstu	uproar
rufu	broke-up, tore-up

S, s

Old Norse	English
sá	saw, so, that
sægarpr	sea-champion
sækja	seek, sought
sæmð	honour
sæmðar	honour
sæmðir	honour
Sæmundi	Saemund (name)
Sæmundur	Saemund (name)
sætt	settled
sættast	reconcile
sættir	reconciliation
sættirnar	reconciliation
sætu	reconcile
sagði	said, said
sagt	said, said, told
sakar	sake
sakir	sake
sáluhjápar	souls
sálum	souls
sama	same
saman	altogether, together
sami	same
samt	the-same, together
sanni	the-truth
sannligast	truthfully
sannyrði	true-words
sárir	wounded
sat	sat
satt	TRUE
sáttarfund	peace-meeting
sáttarfundinum	reconciliation-meeting
sáttargerð	settlement
sátu	sat
sauminn	the-seam
sé	are, being, him, is, they-are, this, to-be
segið	say
segir	said, say, says
segja	say
seinka	delay
sekðir	penalty
sem	as
senda	send
sendi	sent
sendiligstan	to-be-sent
sér	as, him, himself, them, themselves
sett	sat, set, settled
setti	set
settr	set
settust	sat
sex	six
síðan	then
síðar	later
síðast	last
sígast	sinking
sigldu	sailed
sigr	victory
Sigurði	Sigurd (name)
Sigurðr	Sigurd (name)
sik	him, himself
Símon	Simon (name)
Símonar	Simon (name)
símoni	Simon (name), Simon's (name)
sín	him, his, theirs
sína	his, their, themselves
sinn	his, theirs
sinna	his, theirs
sinni	his, they
síns	his
sínu	his, theirs
sínum	his, theirs
sitja	sit
sitt	his, this
sjá	saw, see
sjálfs	himself
sjálft	itself
sjást	looked
skal	shall
skála	cabin
skáladyrrnar	the-door
skálann	the-cabin, the-hut

Word List (Old Norse to English)

Old Norse	English
skálanum	the-cabin
skammt	a-short-distance
skaplyndi	temper
skapraun	temperament
skerast	cutting
skilðu	parted, separated
skilja	part
skip	ship
skipa	the-ships
skipi	ship, the-ship
skipinu	the-ship
skipit	ship, the-ship
skips	ships, the-ships
skiptu	divided
skipum	ships, the-ship
skipverjar	crew
Skjálgsbúða	Skjalgsbud (place)
skjótliga	shortly
skjótt	away
skreið	fish
skulu	shall, would
skyldi	should, should-be
skyldir	should
skyldu	should, would
skyli	shall
slær	struck
slæst	slipped
slátrgripa	carcasses
sleit	tore-up
slembidjákn	the-false-deacon
slík	such
slíka	such
slíkan	such
slíks	such
slíkt	such
slíku	such
slíkum	such
slógu	strike
smáskipum	small-ships
smjörs	of-butter
snaraðist	caught-up
snerist	turned
snúast	return
sofa	sleep
sofnaði	slept
sögðu	said
sögu	saga
Sokka	Sokki (name)
Sokkason	son-of-Sokki (name)
Sokki	Sokki (name)
Sólarfjöllum	Solarfjoll (place)
son	son
söng	sang
sonr	son
sóttu	sought
spangabrynja	plate-mail
spillt	damaged
spretta	sprang
spurði	learned
spurðist	heard-of
spurðu	heard-of
spurðust	heard-of
spurt	learned
spyrjast	known-about
stað	stand
staðar	stand
staðarins	of-the-place, the-place
staðit	stood
stakk	thrust
standa	stand
standist	to-stand
stefnur	plans
steig	stepped
steinda	stone-one
Steingrímr	Steingrim (name)
Steingríms	Steingrim's (name)
steint	stone-carving
Steinþórr	Steinthor (name)
stendr	standing
sterkr	strong
stóð	standing, stood
stofuna	sitting-room
stokk	a-log
stökki	blood-splattered
stól	seat
stórfjörðu	large-fjords
stórir	badly
stórskipum	large-ships
stórvirki	great-works
studdist	stood

Word List (Old Norse to English)

Old Norse	English
stukku	went-away
stutt	supported
stýrimaðr	steersman
stýrimanns	steersman
styrkðarmaðr	supporter
sú	so
suðr	south
sumarit	summer
sumars	summer
sumir	some
sumri	of-summer
sumur	summers
sunnan	to-the-south
svá	so
svara	answered
svarar	answered
svardaga	oath
sveit	company, the-company
sveitunga	men-company
sverði	to-the-sword
sveri	swear
sviptr	deprived
svívirðing	disgrace
svívirðliga	disgracefully
svörð	skins
syfjar	sleepy
sýndi	showed
sýndist	seemed
syngja	sing, sung
sýnir	showed
sýnist	seems
sýnt	shown
systursonr	sister's-son

T, t

Old Norse	English
taka	take, took
tala	spoke
talaði	told
tannvöru	walrus-tusks
tekinn	taken
tekit	taken
tekna	taken
teknir	taken
tíða	the-service
tíðamanni	worshippers
tíðenda	news
tíðendi	news, tidings
tíðendin	the-news
tíðendum	news
tigi	tens
tigir	tens
tignar	position
til	the, to, until
tilstilli	agency, guidance
tindinn	pin
tjáði	spoke, told, voiced
tjald	tent
tjalda	tent-up
tók	took
tóku	took
tólf	twelve
tóm	time
tómliga	time-like
torsóttligt	difficult
traust	trust
troða	tread
tvau	two
tveim	two
týnzt	lost

Þ, þ

Old Norse	English
þá	them, then, when
þakði	covered
þakkaði	thanked
þangat	from-then, from-there
þann	that, then
þannig	that-way
þar	here, that, then, there
þat	it, that, the, this, to
þau	then, those
þegar	instantly, straightaway, straight-away, them
þeim	of-them, theirs, them, they, to-them
þeir	they, was

Word List (Old Norse to English)

Old Norse	English
þeira	of-them, theirs, them, they
þeirar	their
þennan	then
þér	to-you, you
þess	this
þessa	this
þessi	these, this
þessir	these
þessu	this
þessum	these, this
þetta	it, that, this
þiggja	accepted
þik	you
þín	your
þína	yours
þing	assembly
þings	assembly, the-assembly
þjónustumenn	servants-of
þó	though
Þóarinn	Thorarin (name)
Þórarinn	Thorarin (name)
Þórðar	Thord (name)
Þórðarson	son-of-Thord (name)
Þórði	Thord's (name)
Þórðr	Thord (name)
Þorfinns	Thorfin (name)
Þorgils	Thorgils (name)
Þóris	Thori (name)
Þórisson	son-of-Thorri (name)
Þorljótsson	son-of-Thorljot (name)
þótt	though
þótti	thought
þóttumst	thought
þriðja	third, thirdly
þrír	three
þrjá	three
þú	you
þungligar	the-more-difficult
þungs	heavily
þungt	unhappy
þvá	washed
þverra	running-out
því	according, accordingly, as, because, because-of, that, then, therefore, they
þykkir	seems
þykkist	seems
þyrfti	needed

U, u

Old Norse	English
ullkamb	wool-comb
um	about, around
umdæmi	about-judgement
umdæmis	area
ummæli	about-matter
umræða	discussed
una	content
undan	away-from
undarligt	strange
undir	submit, under
uni	like
unna	win
unum	among
upp	up
uppgefnir	up-given
uppi	up
urðu	became

Ú, ú

Old Norse	English
úfar	misfortune
út	out
úti	outside
útlenda	foreign

V, v

Old Norse	English
vægja	make-peace
vænlig	hopeful
vænta	hoped
vænti	expect
væntu	expected

Word List (Old Norse to English)

Old Norse	English
væri	be, should-be, should-they, to-be, was
vættir	weights
vaknaði	awoke
vald	power
ván	expect, expected, hope
vanda	problem
vandi	custom
vanfærr	unable
vanizt	custom
vanmeginn	weak
vápnaðir	weaponed
var	was, were
vár	spring, us
varð	became, came
varða	happen
varist	weariness
várit	spring
várkunn	pity
varla	hardly
várn	our, ours
varnarmaðr	defender
varning	wares
várr	our, ours
várri	ours
váru	was, were
varúðgir	cautious
vaskir	brave
veðr	weather
vegna	slain
veiðiskap	hunting
veit	know, knowing
veita	grant
veitti	granted
veizlu	feast
veizlunni	the-feast
vel	well
veld	willed
veldr	brought-about, caused
vér	us, we, we-are
vera	be, being, to-be, would-be
verð	deserve
verða	be, become
verði	be
verðið	become
verðir	being
verðr	becomes
verit	been
verk	work
verum	we
vestan	western
Vestribyggð	Vestribyggd (place)
Vestribyggðar	Vestribyggd (place)
vetrinn	winter
við	by, to, with
víða	widely
viðbúnað	preparation
viðinn	the-trees
víg	killings, slaying
vígði	consecrated
Víghvats	Vighvats (name)
vígi	battle
vígit	killing
vígsgengi	in-battle
vil	will, wish
vildi	wanted, willed
vildu	willed
vilja	willed, wished-for
viljum	wish
villt	wildly
vini	friends
vinsæll	popular
virðim	worthiness
virðing	worthiness
virðingar	worthiness
virðr	respected
vís	aware
vissu	know
vist	resources
víst	certainly
vistaföng	resources
vistir	supplies
vistunum	provisions
vit	with
vitr	wise
vitrliga	wise-like
vitrum	wise

Word List (Old Norse to English)

Old Norse	English
vitum	know-we
völlinn	the-field

Y, y

yðr	you
yðru	your
yðvar	you, yours
yðvarn	with-you
yfir	over
yfirbóta	over-compensation
yrði	be, become, would

Ý, ý

ýldu	decay

Word List *(English to Old Norse)*

English	Old Norse	English	Old Norse
A, a		also	ok
		altogether	saman
a	á, at, einn	a-man	maðr, mann
a-bear	bjarndýri	among	unum
ability	getu	an-axe	öxi
a-bishop	byskup	and	á, en, enda, er, í, ok
about	á, í, um	angry	illa, óðir, reiðisvipr, reiðr
about-judgement	umdæmi		
about-matter	ummæli	another	annat, annat, öðru
above	ofan	answered	svara, svarar
a-case	mál	anything-else	annat
accepted	þiggja	archbishop	erkibyskups
according	því	are	er, eru, eruð, sé
accordingly	því	area	umdæmis
actually	raunar	are-they	eru
a-deal	kaupum	Arnald (name)	Arnald, Arnaldr
advice	ráð, ráða, ráðum	Arnbjarn (name)	Arnbjarnar
advisable	ráð, ráðligt	Arnbjarnar (name)	Arnbjarnar
advise	ráðist	Arnbjorn (name)	Arnbjörn
a-falsehood	fals	around	um
a-farm	bæ	arrange	ráðast
a-farmer	bóndi	as	á, er, sem, sér, því
a-friendly	mannvænlegr	as-far	nær
after	áðr, eftir	a-short-distance	skammt
afterwards	eftir	asked	bað, báðu, bæði
agency	tilstilli	asked-for	bauð
a-glacier	jöklinum	as-long-as	meðan
a-great	mikit	assembly	þing, þings
agreed	játtuðu	assistance	fulltingis, greiða
a-Greenlander	grænlenzkr	at	á, at, í
a-headed-ship	höfðaskip	autumn	haustum
aided	duga	aware	vís
alike	líka, líkendi	away	brott, brottu, skjótt
all	alla, allan, allir, allir, allt, öllu, öllum	away-from	frá, undan
		awoke	vaknaði
all-great	allmjök	a-word	orð
allow	leggja	a-wound	áverka
all-prepared	albúnir	axe	öx, öxi
all-well	allvel, allvel	axe-horn	öxarhyrnunni
a-log	stokk		
alone	eigi, einn, einni	**B, b**	
alone-going	einangr		

Word List (English to Old Norse)

English	Old Norse
back	aftr, bak
badly	mæla, stórir
battle	bardaga, vígi
be	er, gera, væri, vera, verða, verði, yrði
bear	bera, berast
bearing	byrrinn
be-arranged	ráðast
be-called	heita
became	gerðist, urðu, varð
because	því
because-of	því
become	orðit, verða, verðið, yrði
becomes	verðr
be-compensated	bæta
be-done	gera
been	gengit, verit
before	áðr, fyrir
before-done	fyrirgert
behold	lízt
being	sé, vera, verðir
below	neðan
beside	hjá
best	bezt
better	betr
between	milli
bid	bað, beiddi
bidding	bæn
bishop	byskup, byskups
bishop-less	byskupslaust
bishop's-appointment	byskupsvígslu
bishop's-seat	byskupsstóll, byskupsstólsins
Bjarn (name)	Bjarna
blood-splattered	stökki
boards	borð
boat-lose	bótalausir
bodies	líkum
boiling-cauldrons	heitukötlum
bones	bein, beinum
booth	búð
bore	bar
bore-up	borðit
borne	borit
both	báðir

English	Old Norse
bothered	nenna
Brand (name)	Brandr
Brattahlid (place)	Brattahlíð
brave	vaskir
breach-of-oath	eiðrofa
break-open	rjúfa
briefs	bréfum
bring	færa
broken	brotit
broke-up	rufu
brother	bróðir
brought	borin, borit, færði
brought-about	veldr
buck	bokki
burned	brenndu
but	eða, en, enn, er
by	at, hjá, við

C, c

English	Old Norse
cabin	skála
call	hringja, kalla
called	hringði, kallaði, kallar, kveðja
came	kom, komast, komst, kómu, kómust, varð
can	kann
captivity	fangs
carcasses	slátrgripa
carried	báru, borinn
carry	heimta
case	mál, málum
cases	málum"
cast	kastaði
caught-up	snaraðist
caused	veldr
cautious	varúðgir
certainly	víst
chest	brögð
chieftains	höfðingja
choice	kostr
church	kirkju
church-mass	kirkjumessu
church-wall	kirkjuvegginn
churchyard	kirkjugarðsins

Word List (English to Old Norse)

English	Old Norse	English	Old Norse
circumstances	hag	deserve	verð
claim	kalla	desirable	agir
clear-dreams	berdreyman	desire	fýsa
cleric	klerkr	did	gerði, gerðu
close	nær	died	andaðist, andaðist
clump	hríslu	difficult	erfitt, torsóttligt
comb	kambi	discharge	hleypið
come	kemst, koma, komast, kominn, komit	discuss	máli
		discussed	umræða
comes	kæmi	disease	mein
coming	kominn	disgrace	svívirðing
commanded	réð	disgracefully	svívirðliga
companions	félaga, félagar	dishonourable	ósæmð, óþekkðarsvip
company	liði, sveit	divided	skiptu
compensation	greiðslu	do	gera
consecrated	vígði	doing	gera
content	una	done	gera, gerðu, gert, gerzt
coolly	fáliga		
correctness	réttligast	down	niðr
court	dómi	downhill	forbrekkis
covered	þakði	dream	draum
crags	hamarrifu	dreamed	dreymði
crew	skipverjar	drifted	rak
custom	vandi, vanizt	drove	rak
cutting	skerast	drowned	drukknaði
		dwelling	bænum

D, d

E, e

English	Old Norse	English	Old Norse
damaged	spillt		
dangerous	mannhættu	each	hvárrtveggi, hvárt, hváru, hvárum, hverr
dead	dauða, dauðr		
dead-body	mannshræ	earthed	jarða
deal	réðist	earth-house	jarðhús
death	bana	Eastern-man	austmaðr
death-blow	banahögg	Eastern-men	austmanna, austmenn
death-wounds	banasár		
decay	ýldu	Eid (place)	Eiði
decide	ráð	Einar (name)	Einar, Einari, Einarr, Einars
declared	kveðit		
decreased	minnka	Einar's	einars
deemed	dæma	Einar's (name)	Einars
defender	varnarmaðr	Einarsfjord (place)	Einarsfjörð
delay	seinka	either-side	hvárirtveggja, hvárirtveggju
Denmark (place)	Danmarkar, Danmörk		
deprived	sviptr	empty	autt
		ends	lýkr

Word List (English to Old Norse)

English	Old Norse
equal	jafnt
equally-early	jafnsnemma
equal-man	mannjafnað
equipment	búnaði, búnaðr
Eriksfjord (place)	Eiríksfjörð
errand	erendi, erendis
esteem	metorð
even	jöfn
events	atburði
execution	framkvæmð
expect	vænti, ván
expected	væntu, ván
Eyjafjolls (place)	Eyjafjöllum

F, f

English	Old Norse
facing	móti
fair	ferlig
fall	falla
fallen	fallinn
far	fjarri
farmer	bónda, bóndi
farmers	bændr
father-and-son	feðgar
feast	veizlu
fee-gifts	fégjöfum
feet	fótum
fee-trust	féván
fell	fell
fifteen	fimmtán
fight	berjast
find	hitta
fire-place	eldstóar
first	fyrst
firstly	fyrst
fish	skreið
fix	festa
fjord	fjörðinn
flesh	holdi
folk	fólk
follow	fylgði
followed	eftir, fylgði, fylgir
following	eftir, fylgðinni
following-men	fjölmenni
food	mat

English	Old Norse
for	fór, fyrir, fyrr
force	liðskost
foreign	útlenda
foremost	fyrir
foresight	forsjá
foster-brother	fóstbróðir
found	fundit, fundu, hitti, hittust
found-out	fréttu
friends	vini
from	af, af, frá, fram, frammi, ór
from-then	þangat
from-there	þangat
fulfil	fulltingja
funeral-procession	líkhringingu

G, g

English	Old Norse
gain	aflat
Gardar (place)	garða, Görðum
gave	gaf, gafst
gave-him	reyndust
get	fá, get, næði
getting	náir
giants	rísi
give	gefa, gefast
given	gefizt, gefnar
glaciers	jöklum
go	fari, farim, ganga
god's	guðs
going	færi, fara, farit, ganga, gengit, göngu
good	góð, góða, góðan, góðr, gott
good-bargain	hagkeypi
good-will	góðgirnd
got	fekk, fékk, fengu
go-to	færi
grant	veita
granted	veitti
grave	grafa
great	mikil, mikill, mikit, mikla
great-works	stórvirki

Word List (English to Old Norse)

English	Old Norse
Greenland (place)	grænland, Grænlendinga, Grænlendingum
Greenlanders (name)	grænlendinga, grænlendingar, grænlendingum
Greenlandic (name)	grænlenzk, grænlenzkum
grouped	flokk
guidance	tilstilli

H, h

English	Old Norse
had	ætti, átt, áttu, hafa, hafði, hafi, haft, hefði, höfðu, lét, létu, lézt
had-they	höfðu
Hall (name)	Hallr
Hall's	halls
Hall's (name)	Halls
hammer	hnjóðhamar
hand	hendi, hendr, hönd
handling	höndum
handy	hagr
happen	varða
Harald (name)	haraldi, haralds
hardly	varla
harm	mein
harmed	harmaði
has	hafa, haft, hefir
has-been	hafa
have	áttu, eiga, hafa, hafið, hefi, hefir, höfum, leggja
have-become	orðit
he	hann, honum
head	höfði, höfuð
headland	nes
head-men	höfuðsmenn
head-ship	höfðaskipit
headstrong	höfuðgjarnt
hear	heyra
heard	heyrðu, heyrt
heard-of	spurðist, spurðu, spurðust
heavily	þungs
held	heldu, héldu
help	fulltings
here	hér, hingat, þar
Hermund (name)	Hermundr
hidden-creek	leynivági
hiding	dyljast
high-mass	hámessu
him	hann, hans, honum, sé, sér, sik, sín
himself	sér, sik, sjálfs
his	hans, honum, sín, sína, sinn, sinna, sinni, síns, sínu, sínum, sitt
his-mind	hugi
hold	halda, haldi
holding	haldit
Holtavatnsos (place)	Holtavatnsós
home	heim
homelands	ættjarða
honour	sæmð, sæmðar, sæmðir
hope	ván
hoped	vænta
hopeful	vænlig
house	húsa
house-man	heimamaðr
how	hverju
how-so	hversu
human-body	mannshræ
humility	lítillæti
hunting	veiðiskap
Hvitserk (name)	Hvítserk

I, i

English	Old Norse
I	ek, mér
ice	ís, ísinn
Iceland (place)	íslandi, íslands
if	ef
ill	illa, illt, öllum
important	metnir
impulsive	óforsjáll
in	á, at, er, í, inn, inni
in-battle	vígsgengi

Word List (English to Old Norse)

English	Old Norse
innermost	leyndust
instantly	þegar
intend	ætla
intended	ætla, ætlaðir
intention	ætlan
in-the-grave	grafin
into	í
invited	bauð
is	er, sé
Isa-Steingrim (name)	Ísa-Steingrímr
is-named	heitir
it	at, er, þat, þetta
its	hans
itself	sjálft

J, j

English	Old Norse
jerk	kippim
Jerusalem-Traveller (name)	Jórsalafari
journey	ferð
judged	dæmði
judgement	dómr

K, k

English	Old Norse
Ketil (name)	Ketil, Ketill, Ketils
Ketil's (name)	Ketils
Kidjaberg (place)	Kiðjabergs
killed	bana
killing	dráp, drepa, vígit
killings	víg
kinsman	frænda, frændi, frændr
kinsmen	frændr
knees	knjám
know	veit, vissu
knowing	veit
known	kunni, kunnig
known-about	spyrjast
know-we	vitum
Kolbein (name)	Kolbein, Kolbeini, Kolbeinn, Kolbeins
Krak (name)	Kráks

L, l

English	Old Norse
laid	lagðist, lagðr, legit, lét, lögðu
laid-out	lét
land	land
lands-men	landsmenn, landsmönnum
Langanes (place)	Langanes
large	mikla
large-fjords	stórfjörðu
large-ships	stórskipum
last	síðast
later	eftir, síðar
law	lög, lögum
laws	lög
lay	lá, leggja
lay-out	láta
learned	fróði, spurði, spurt
less	minni, mun
lessened	menn
like	líka, líkar, uni
liked	líkaði
likely	líkast, líkligast
likes	líkar
little	lítil, lítit, litlu, lítt
lived	bjó
loaded	hlaðna
local-priest	heimilisprestr
long	lengi
longer	lengr, lengra
looked	horfðu, leit, sjást
looks	horfir
loss-of-life	líftjóni
lost	misst, týnzt
lot	hlut, hlutar
Lund (place)	Lundi

M, m

English	Old Norse
made	gerðir, gert
make	gera, gerir
make-peace	vægja

Word List (English to Old Norse)

English	Old Norse
man	maðr, mann, manni
man's	manna
many	margt, mikit
many-people	fjölmenni
mass	messu
matter	mál, málum
matter-lot	málahlutr
matters	mál
may	mega, munu
me	mér, mik
meagre	megri
meanness	manndómsleysi
meet	fund, fundar, mót
meeting	fund, fundar, mót
men	manna, menn, mönnum
men-company	sveitunga
merchant-ship	kaupskip, kaupskipit
merchant-ships	kaupskipin
met	hitti, hittust
might	mætti, mættir, mátti
mind	hugr
mine	mér, mín, minn, minni, mínum
misfortune	úfar
moderately	meðallagi
money	fjár
month's-end	mánaðarmótit
more	fleiri, meir, meira, meiri
more-correct	réttara
morning	morgininn
most	makligast, mest
mouth	munni
much	mikil, mikill, mikils, mikinn, mikit, mikla, miklir, miklu, mjök
my	mínum, mitt

N, n

English	Old Norse
named	hét
nature	eðli
nearer	nær
necessary	nauðsyn
needed	þyrfti
needs	nauðsyn
news	tíðenda, tíðendi, tíðendum
next	næst
night	kveld, nætr, nátt
no	eigi, engi, engum
none	ekki
no-one	engi
nor	né
Nordic (name)	norrænir, norrænn
Norway (place)	Nóreg, nóregi, Nóregs
not	eiga, eigi, ekki, nú
now	nú

O, o

English	Old Norse
oath	eið, eiðar, svardaga
Odda (place)	Odda
of	á, af, af, at, ef, í, of
of-butter	smjörs
off	af
offer	bjóðast
offering	boðit
of-men	manna
of-mind	æðimaðr
of-old	forn
of-Ossur (name)	Özurar
of-summer	sumri
often	oft
of-them	þeim, þeira
of-the-place	staðarins
old	gamall
old-woman	kerling
on	á, í
one	ein, eina, einn, einu, einum, enn
one-occasion	einhverju
opinion	fastmæli
opposite	gegnt
or	eða
Ossur (name)	Özur, Özurar, Özuri, Özurr
other	aðrir, annarra, annat, öðru, öðrum

Word List (English to Old Norse)

English	Old Norse	English	Old Norse
other-either	annathvárt	prevented	bægði
others	hinir, öðrum	pride	dignuðu
otherwise	annat	priest	guði
our	várn, várr	priests	kennimenn
ours	várn, várr, várri	problem	vanda
out	á, út	promised	hézt
out-from	ór	property	eign, eigna
out-of	ór	propose	leggr
outside	úti	protect	hlífast
over	ofan, yfir	protected	hegna
overbearing-men	ofsamenn	provided	fremi
over-compensation	yfirbóta	provisions	fanga, feng, vistunum
own	eiga	pulled	kippðu
owned	átt	punish	refsa
owning	eignum	put	legðu

P, p

R, r

English	Old Norse	English	Old Norse
part	hlut, skilja	ran	hleypr, hljóp, hlupu
parted	skilðu	rather	halda, heldr
pass	gegna	reached	náðu
passed	liðit, líðr, liðu	reconcile	sættast, sætu
paying	greiðist	reconciliation	sættir, sættirnar
payment	gjalds	reconciliation-meeting	sáttarfundinum
peace	fritt	refusing	fyrirkveðast
peace-meeting	sáttarfund	released	hleypir, leysti
penalty	sekðir	reluctant	ófúss
people	menn	remaining	eftir
peoples'	manna	remember	muna
pin	tindinn	repel	hrinda
pity	várkunn	rescue	bjargar
plan	atgervi	rescuing	bjarga
plans	stefnur	residence	gilla
plate-mail	spangabrynja	resources	fang, föngum, vist, vistaföng
poor-man	ómegðarmaðr	respected	virðr
popular	vinsæll	return	snúast
position	tignar	reward	laun
possible	auðit	right	hægra
power	vald	rights	rétt
prayers	bæn, bænar	river-mouth	árós
preparation	viðbúnað	rocks	björg
preparations	búnað, búnaði	rode	reið
prepared	bjó, bjóst, búa, búinn, búit, búnir, býr	ruled	réðst
presented	borit, heimti	running	hlaupa

Word List (English to Old Norse)

English	Old Norse	English	Old Norse
running-out	þverra	should	mun, mundu, muni, munu, skyldi, skyldir, skyldu

S, s

English	Old Norse	English	Old Norse
		should-be	skyldi, væri
		shoulders	herða
Saemund (name)	Sæmundi, Sæmundur	should-they	væri
saga	sögu	shouting	æpa
said	kvað, kvaðst, kváðu, kváðust, kveðst, mælti, mæltu, sagði, sagði, sagt, sagt, segir, sögðu	showed	sýndi, sýnir
		shown	sýnt
		shrubs	hrísótt
		sides	megin
		Sigurd (name)	Sigurði, Sigurðr
sailed	sigldu	Simon (name)	Símon, Símonar, símoni
sake	sakar, sakir		
same	sama, sami	Simon's (name)	Símoni
sang	söng	sing	syngja
sat	sat, sátu, sett, settust	sinking	sígast
satisfactory	hlítt	sir	herra
saw	sá, sjá	sister's-son	systursonr
say	segið, segir, segja	sit	sitja
saying	kváðu	sitting-room	stofuna
says	segir	six	sex
sea	haf	skins	svörð
sea-champion	sægarpr	Skjalgsbud (place)	Skjálgsbúða
sea-going-ship	hafskip	slain	vegna
seals	innsiglum	slander	róg
seat	stól	slaying	víg
see	sjá	sleep	sofa
seek	leita, sækja	sleepy	syfjar
seemed	sýndist	slept	sofnaði
seems	sýnist, þykkir, þykkist	slipped	slæst
self-will	einræði	small-ships	smáskipum
send	senda	so	sá, sú, svá
sent	sendi	Sokki (name)	Sokka, Sokki
separated	skilðu	Solarfjoll (place)	Sólarfjöllum
servants-of	þjónustumenn	solution	órræði, órræðit
set	sett, setti, settr	some	nökkur, nökkura, nökkurar, nökkurn, nökkuru, nökkurum, nökkut, sumir
settled	bjó, búit, sætt, sett		
settlement	sáttargerð		
shall	muni, munum, skal, skulu, skyli		
		something	nökkurra
		son	son, sonr
shall-you	muntu	son-of-Kalf (name)	Kálfsson
she	hún	son-of-Kodran (name)	Koðránsson
ship	skip, skipi, skipit	son-of-Njal (name)	Njálsson
ships	skips, skipum	son-of-Sokki (name)	Sokkason
shortly	skjótliga		

Word List (English to Old Norse)

English	*Old Norse*	*English*	*Old Norse*
son-of-Thord (name)	Þórðarson		
son-of-Thorljot (name)	Þorljótsson	**T, t**	
son-of-Thorri (name)	Þórisson	take	taka
sought	sækja, sóttu	taken	tekinn, tekit, tekna, teknir
souls	sáluhjápar, sálum	taking	nema
south	suðr	teaching	kennimanns
spoke	mælti, tala, tjáði	team	lið, liði
sprang	spretta	temper	skaplyndi
spring	vár, várit	temperament	skapraun
stand	stað, staðar, standa	tens	tigi, tigir
standing	stendr, stóð	tent	tjald
steersman	stýrimaðr, stýrimanns	tent-up	tjalda
Steingrim (name)	Steingrímr	than	en
Steingrim's (name)	Steingríms	thanked	þakkaði
Steinthor (name)	Steinþórr	that	á, áðu, at, er, hvat, í, sá, þann, þar, þat, þetta, því
stepped	steig		
still	enn, kyrrlátir, kyrrt	that-way	þannig
stone-carving	steint	the	á, at, er, inn, inu, it, þat, til
stone-one	steinda		
stood	staðit, stóð, studdist	the-after-boat	eftirbátinn
stormy	hvasst	the-animal	dýrit
straightaway	þegar	the-archbishop	erkibyskup
straight-away	þegar	the-armour	brynjunni
strange	undarligt	the-artefact-fee	gripagjaldit
strengthened	efldr	the-assembly	þings
strike	slógu	the-bishop	byskup, byskupi, byskups
strong	sterkr		
struck	hjó, höggvit, slær	the-bishop-elect	byskupsefni
submit	undir	the-bishop's	byskups
such	slík, slíka, slíkan, slíks, slíkt, slíku, slíkum	the-bishop's-seat	byskupsstólinum, byskupsstólnum
suitable	henta	the-boat	bátinn
summer	sumarit, sumars	the-boat-behind	eftirbáti
summers	sumur	the-body	lík, líkinu
sung	syngja	the-branch	hríslunni
supplies	vistir	the-cabin	skálann, skálanum
support	liðveizlu	the-case	mál, málit
supported	stutt	the-church	kirkju, kirkjuna
supporter	styrkðarmaðr	the-company	sveit
suppose	ætla	the-court	dómi, dóminum
supposed	ætla, ætluðu	the-crew	hásetar
swear	sveri	the-day	dag
swiftly	ört	the-dead	daun
		the-door	hurðina, skáladyrrnar

Word List (English to Old Norse)

English	Old Norse
the-dream	drauminn
the-dwelling	bænum
the-Easterner	austmanns
the-fairest	fagra
the-false-deacon	slembidjákn
the-feast	veizlunni
the-ferry	ferjuna
the-field	völlinn
the-fjord	fjörðu
the-funeral-procession	líkhringingina
the-Greenlander	grænlendings
the-Greenlanders	grænlendingar
the-Greenlanders'	grænlendinga
the-Hermunds (name)	Hermundr
the-hut	skálann
their	sína, þeirar
theirs	sín, sinn, sinna, sínu, sínum, þeim, þeira
the-judgement	dómrinn
the-keel	kilinum
the-kind	konungi
the-king	konung, konungi, konungr, konungs
the-king's	konungs
the-king's-brief	konungsbréfum
the-land	landi, landit
the-Landeys (place)	Landeyjum
the-lands	landsins
them	sér, þá, þegar, þeim, þeira
the-man	mann
the-matter	mal, mál, máli, málum, málunum
the-matter-fulfilling	málsfyllingar
the-men	mönnum
the-merchants	kaupmenn
the-middle	miðju
the-more-difficult	þungligar
the-most	mestr
themselves	sér, sína
then	er, it, síðan, þá, þann, þar, þau, þennan, því
the-news	tíðendin
the-night	nætr, nótt
the-old-woman	kerlingu
the-place	staðarins
there	þar
therefore	því
the-same	samt
these	þessi, þessir, þessum
the-seam	sauminn
the-service	tíða
the-settlement	byggðina
the-ship	skipi, skipinu, skipit, skipum
the-ships	skipa, skips
the-slope	brekku, brekkunni
the-storm	andviðri
the-table	borðit
the-tables	borð, borðum
the-trading-men	kaupmenn, kaupmennirnir, kaupmönnum
the-trees	viðinn
the-trunk	bolöx
the-truth	sanni
the-unsettled-land	óbyggðum
the-way	leið
the-words	orðinn
they	sinni, þeim, þeir, þeira, því
they-are	eru, sé
they-had	höfðu
things	hlutum
think	hygg
third	þriðja
thirdly	þriðja
this	sé, sitt, þat, þess, þessa, þessi, þessu, þessum, þetta
this-man	manninum
Thorarin (name)	Þóarinn, Þórarinn
Thord (name)	Þórðar, Þórðr
Thord's (name)	Þórði
Thorfin (name)	Þorfinns
Thorgils (name)	Þorgils
Thori (name)	Þóris
those	þau
though	þó, þótt
thought	hugðu, þótti, þóttumst
three	þrír, þrjá
throat	barkann

Word List (English to Old Norse)

English	Old Norse	English	Old Norse
through	fyrir, gegnum	unable	vanfærr
thrust	stakk	uncertain	óvíst
tidings	tíðendi	uncompensated	óbættr
time	hríð, tóm	under	undir
time-like	tómliga	unequal	ójafnaðr
to	á, at, fyrir, í, þat, til, við	un-equal	ójafnað
		ungraceful	óþekkðarsvip
to-be	sé, væri, vera	unhappy	þungt
to-be-sent	sendiligstan	unheard-of	endemi
to-catch	fangit	unsettled	ósett
to-do	gera, gerðu	un-settled	óbyggðir
together	saman, samt	until	til
to-give	gera	un-worthy	óvirðing
to-him	honum	up	upp, uppi
to-hold	halda	up-given	uppgefnir
told	mælt, sagt, talaði, tjáði	uproar	róstu
		upset	brugðit
to-me	mér	us	oss, vár, vér
took	taka, tók, tóku	use	nytjum
tore-up	rufu, sleit		
to-stand	standist		
to-strike	höggva		

V, v

English	Old Norse
to-them	þeim
to-the-south	sunnan
to-the-sword	sverði
to-us	oss
to-you	þér
trading-men	kaupmenn, kaupmönnum
travel	færi, færim, fara, fórum
travelled	fór, fóru, fórum
tread	troða
treasure	gersemi, gripi, gripina
true	

English	Old Norse
valid	gildr
very	mjök
Vestribyggd (place)	Vestribyggð, Vestribyggðar
victory	sigr
Vighvats (name)	Víghvats
violence	ofsa
voiced	tjáði

W, w

English	Old Norse
true-words	sannyrði
trust	traust
truthfully	sannligast
turn	hverfa
turned	snerist
twelve	tólf
two	tvau, tveim

English	Old Norse
walked	gengit
walrus-tusks	tannvöru
wandered	reikaði
wanted	vildi
wares	varning
was	er, þeir, væri, var, váru
washed	þvá
was-named	hét
way	brott, burt
we	vér, verum

U, u

Word List (English to Old Norse)

English	*Old Norse*
weak	fallinn, vanmeginn
wealth	fé, féit
wealth-finding	fjárfundinn
weaponed	vápnaðir
we-are	er, vér
weariness	varist
weather	veðr
weights	vættir
well	vel
went	fara, fara, fekk, ferr, fór, fóru, ganga, gekk, gengr, gengu
went-away	stukku
were	eru, var, váru
western	vestan
what	er, hvat
when	er, þá
where	er, horfir, hvar
whether	hvárt
which	hvárs
while	en, meðan
white-bear	hvítabjörn
who	er, hverr
widely	víða
wildly	villt
will	mun, muni, vil
will-be	mun
willed	veld, vildi, vildu, vilja
willing	fúsari
win	unna
winter	vetrinn
wise	vitr, vitrum
wise-like	vitrliga
wish	vil, viljum
wished-for	vilja
with	er, með, við, vit
with-you	yðvarn
wool-comb	ullkamb
word	orð
words	orð, orða
word-sending	orðsending
work	verk
worshippers	tíðamanni
worthiness	virðim, virðing, virðingar
would	mun, mundi, mundu, muni, munt, munu, myndim, skulu, skyldu, yrði
would-be	mundu, vera
would-get	fengi
wounded	sárir

Y, y

English	*Old Norse*
you	þér, þik, þú, yðr, yðvar
your	þín, yðru
yours	þína, yðvar

The Tale of the Greenlanders (II) (The Tale of Einarr Sokkason) (*Old Icelandic*)

Old Icelandic	Literal	English
1	**1**	**1**
Sokki hét maður og var Þórisson.	Sokki was-named a-man and was Son-of-Thorri.	There was a man named Sokki, and he was the son of Thorri.
Hann bjó í Brattahlíð á Grænlandi.	He lived in Brattahlid in Greenland.	He lived in Brattahlid in Greenland.
Hann var mikils virður og vinsæll.	He was much respected and popular.	He was much respected and popular.
Einar hét son hans og var mannvænlegur maður.	Einar was-named son his and was a-friendly man.	His son was named Einar and he was a friendly man.
Þeir feðgar áttu mikið vald á Grænlandi og voru þeir þar mjög fyrir mönnum.	They father-and-son had great power in Greenland and were they there much foremost men.	The father and son had great power in Greenland and they were prominent men.
Einhverju sinni lét Sokki þings kveðja og tjáði það fyrir mönnum að hann vildi að landið væri eigi lengur biskupslaust og vildi að allir landsmenn legðu sína muni til að biskupsstóll væri efldur.	One-occasion they had Sokki assembly called and voiced that before the-men that he willed that the-land be no longer bishop-less and willed that all lands-men put themselves should to a bishop's-seat to-be strengthened.	On one occasion Sokki had an assembly called and announced before the men that he wished that the land should no longer be without a bishop, and he wished that all the men of the land should contribute towards a bishop's seat to be established.
Bændur játtuðu því allir.	Farmers agreed accordingly all.	Accordingly the farmers agreed to this.
Sokki bað Einar son sinn fara þessa ferð til Noregs, kvað hann vera sendilegastan mann þess erindis að fara.	Sokki bid Einar son his travel this journey to Norway, said he would-be to-be-sent man this errand to travel.	Sokki asked his son Einar to travel on a journey to Norway as the best man for this errand.
Hann kveðst fara mundu sem hann vildi.	He said travel would as he willed.	He said that he would travel as wished.
Einar hafði með sér tannvöru mikla og svörð að heimta sig fram við höfðingja.	Einar had with him walrus-tusks great and skins to carry himself from with chieftains.	Einar had great walrus tusks and skins with him to further his case with the chieftains.

The Tale of the Greenlanders (II) (The Tale of Einarr Sokkason) (Old Icelandic)

Old Icelandic	Literal	English
Þeir komu við Noreg.	They came to Norway.	They came to Norway.
Þá var Sigurður Jórsalafari konungur að Noregi.	Then was Sigurd Jerusalem-Traveller the-king of Norway.	Then Sigurd Jerusalem-farer was king of Norway.
Einar kom á fund konungs og heimti sig fram með fégjöfum og tjáði síðan mál sitt og erindi og beiddi konung þar til fulltings að hann næði slíku sem hann beiddi fyrir nauðsyn landsins.	Einar came to meeting the-king's and presented himself from with fee-gifts and spoke then matters his and errand and bid the-king there to help that he get such as he bid for needs the-lands.	Einar came to have a meeting with the king and presented himself well with wealthy gifts on account of his errand, and asked the king to help him get that which his lands needed.
Konungur lét þeim það víst betur henta.	The-king had them that certainly better suitable.	The king agreed that it would certainly be better suited.
Síðan kallaði konungur til sín þann mann er Arnaldur hét.	Then called the-king to him then a-man was Arnald named.	Then the king called to him a man who was named Arnald.
Hann var góður klerkur og vel til kennimanns fallinn.	He was good cleric and well to teaching fallen.	He was a good cleric and well fallen to teaching.
Konungur beiddi að hann réðist til þessa vanda fyrir guðs sakir og bænar hans "og mun eg senda þig til Danmerkur á fund Össurar erkibiskups í Lund með mínum bréfum og innsiglum".	The-king bid that he deal to this problem for god's sake and prayers his "and will I send you to Denmark to meet Ossur archbishop in Lund with my briefs and seals".	The king asked him to deal with this problem God's sake and his prayers, "And I will send you to Denmark to meet archbishop Ossur of Lund with my letters and seals".
Arnaldur kvaðst ófús til að ráðast, fyrst fyrir sjálfs síns sakir er hann væri lítt til fallinn og síðan að skilja við vini sína og frændur, í þriðja stað að eiga við torsóttlegt fólk.	Arnald said reluctant to that arrange, firstly for himself his sake as he was little to weak and then to part with friends his and kinsmen, and thirdly stand to not with difficult folk.	Arnald said that he was reluctant to arrange this, firstly for his sake because he was ill-fitted for it, and secondly to part with his friends and kinsmen, and thirdly he did not wish to have to talk to such difficult folk.
Konungur kvað hann því meira gott mundu eftir taka sem hann hefði meiri skapraun af mönnum.	The-king said he that more good would afterwards take as he had more temperament of men.	The king said that the more his difficulty at the hands of temperamental men, the greater his reward would be afterwards.

The Tale of the Greenlanders (II) (The Tale of Einarr Sokkason) (Old Icelandic)

Old Icelandic	Literal	English
Hann kveðst eigi nenna að skerast undan hans bæn "en ef þess verður auðið að eg taki biskupsvígslu þá vil eg að Einar sverji mér þess eið að halda og fulltingja rétt biskupsstólsins og eignum þeim er guði eru gefnar og hegna þeim er á ganga og sé varnarmaður fyrir öllum hlutum staðarins".	He said not bothered to cutting away-from his prayers "but if this becomes possible that I take bishop's-appointment then will I that Einar swear to-me this oath to hold and fulfil rights bishop's-seat and owning them the priest are given and protected they are to go and being defender for all things the-place".	He said that he did not want the bother of cutting away from his prayers "but if it becomes possible that I take the appointment of bishop, then I wish Einar to swear to me this oath, to hold and fulfil the rights of the bishop's seat, and all that is given to the priest, and to be the protector and defender of all things to do with the bishop's seat".
Konungur kvað hann það gera skyldu.	The-king said he that to-do should.	The king said that he should do this.
Einar kvaðst mundu undir það ganga.	Einar said would submit to go.	Einar said he would submit to going along with it.
Síðan fór biskupsefni á fund Össurar erkibiskups og sagði honum sitt erindi með konungsbréfum.	Then travelled the-bishop-elect to meet Ossur archbishop and said to-him this errand with the-king's-brief.	Then the bishop-elect went to meet archbishop Ossur and told him of his errand with the king's letters.
Erkibiskup tók honum vel og reyndust hugi við.	The-archbishop took him well and gave-him his-mind with.	The archbishop received him well and gave to him with his mind.
Og er biskup sá að þessi maður var vel til tignar fallinn vígði hann Arnald til biskups og leysti hann vel af hendi.	And when the-bishop saw that this man was well to position fallen consecrated he Arnald to bishop and released him well of hand.	And when the bishop saw that this man was well given to the position he consecrated Arnald to bishop and parted with him warmly.
Síðan kom Arnaldur biskup til konungs og tók hann við honum vel.	Then came Arnald bishop to the-king and took he with him well.	Then bishop Arnald went to the kind and he received him well.
Einar hafði haft með sér bjarndýri af Grænlandi og gaf það Sigurði konungi.	Einar had had with him a-bear from Greenland and gave it Sigurd the-king.	Einar had a bear with him from Greenland and gave it to Sigurd the king.
Fékk hann þar í mót sæmdir og metorð af konungi.	Got he then to meet honour and esteem from the-king.	He then got honour and esteem from the king.
Síðan fóru þeir á einu skipi, biskup og Einar.	Then travelled they on one ship, the-bishop and Einar.	Then they travelled on a ship, the bishop and Einar.

The Tale of the Greenlanders (II) (The Tale of Einarr Sokkason) (Old Icelandic)

Old Icelandic	Literal	English
Á öðru skipi bjóst Arnbjörn austmaður og norrænir menn með honum og vildu og fara út til Grænlands.	On another ship prepared Arnbjorn Eastern-man and Nordic men with him and willed also travel out to Greenland.	Prepared on another ship was Arnbjorn the Norwegian and other Norse men with him who wished to travel to Greenland.
Síðan létu þeir í haf og greiðast eigi byrinn mjög í hag þeim og komu þeir biskup og Einar í Holtavatnsós undir Eyjafjöllum á Íslandi.	Then had they to sea and paying not bearing much of circumstances theirs and came they bishop and Einar to Holtavatnsos under Eyjafjolls in Iceland.	Then they put to sea and the situation was not very favourable for them, and the bishop and Einar arrived in Holtavatnsós under the Eyjafjolls in Iceland.
Þá bjó Sæmundur hinn fróði í Odda.	Then lived Saemund the learned in Odda.	Then Saemund the learned lived in Odda.
Hann fór á fund biskups og bauð honum til sín um veturinn.	He went to meet the-bishop and invited him to his about winter.	He went to see the bishop and invited him to stay with him for the winter.
Biskup þakkaði honum og lést það þiggja mundu.	Bishop thanked him and had that accepted would.	The bishop thanked him and had accepted it.
Einar var undir Eyjafjöllum um veturinn.	Einar was under Eyjafjolls about winter.	Einar was under Eyjafjolls during the winter.
Það er sagt þá er biskup reið frá skipi og menn hans að þeir áðu á bæ nokkurum í Landeyjum og sátu úti.	It is said when that bishop rode from the-ship and men his that they that to a-farm some in The-Landeys and sat outside.	It is said that when the bishop and his men got off the ship, they went to a farm in the Landeys and sat outside.
Þá gekk út kerling ein og hafði ullkamb í hendi.	Then went out old-woman one and had wool-comb in hand.	Then an old woman walked out alone with a wool comb in her hand.
Hún gekk að einum manni og mælti:	She went to one man and said:	She walked up to one man and said:
"Muntu festa, bokki, tindinn í kambi mínum?"	"Shall-you fix, buck, pin in comb mine?"	"Will you fix the pin in my comb, buck?"
Hann tók við og kvaðst mundu að gera og tók hnjóðhamar úr mal einum og gerði að og líkaði kerlingu allvel,	He took with and said would to done and took hammer out-of the-matter one and did it and liked the-old-woman all-well,	He took it over and said that he would do it, and he took a hammer off the ground and did it, and the old woman liked this very well,
en það var biskup raunar.	and it was a-bishop actually.	and it was actually a bishop.

The Tale of the Greenlanders (II) (The Tale of Einarr Sokkason) (Old Icelandic)

Old Icelandic	Literal	English
Hann var hagur vel og er því frá þessu sagt að hann sýndi lítillæti sitt.	He was handy well and was therefore from this said that he showed humility his.	He was very handy and it is told from this of how he showed his humility.
Hann var í Odda um veturinn og fór með þeim Sæmundi allvel.	He was in Odda about winter and went with them Saemund all-well.	He was in Odda during the winter and got on very well with Saemund.
En til þeirra Arnbjarnar spurðist ekki.	But to them Arnbjarn heard-of not.	But they did not hear of Arnbjarn.
Ætluðu þeir biskup að hann mundi kominn til Grænlands.	Supposed they bishop that he would come to Greenland.	They thought the bishop would come to Greenland.
Um sumarið eftir fóru þeir biskup og Einar af Íslandi og komu við Grænland í Eiríksfjörð og tóku menn við þeim allvel.	About summer after went they the-bishop and Einar from Iceland and came to Greenland in Eriksfjord and took men with them all-well.	In the following summer, the bishop and Einar left Iceland and arrived at Greenland in Eriksfjord and were well received by the people.
Spurðu þeir þá enn ekki til Arnbjarnar og þótti það undarlegt og liðu svo nokkur sumur.	Heard-of they then but not to Arnbjarn and thought that strange and passed so some summers.	They still didn't hear about Arnbjarn and thought it was strange, and then a few summers passed.
Gerðist nú á umræða mikil að þeir muni týnst hafa.	Became now of discussed much that they would lost have.	There was now much discussion that they must have been lost.
Biskup setti stól sinn í Görðum og réðst þangað til.	Bishop set seat his in Gardar and ruled from-then to.	The bishop placed his chair in Gardar and ruled until then.
Var Einar honum þá mestur styrktarmaður og þeir feðgar.	Was Einar to-him then the-most supporter and they father-and-son.	Einar was his greatest supporter then, and they were father and son.
Þeir voru og mest metnir af öllum landsmönnum af biskupi.	They were and most important of all lands-men of the-bishop.	They were and the most valued of all the countrymen by the bishop.

2

Sigurður hét maður og var Njálsson, grænlenskur maður.	Sigurd was-named a-man and was Son-of-Njal, a-Greenlander man.	There was a man named Sigurd who was the son of Njal, a Greenlander man.
Hann fór oft á haustum til fangs í óbyggðir.	He travelled often out autumn to captivity in un-settled.	He often went in the fall to captivity in the wilderness.

The Tale of the Greenlanders (II) (The Tale of Einarr Sokkason) (Old Icelandic)

Old Icelandic	Literal	English
Hann var sægarpur mikill.	He was sea-champion much.	He was very much a champion of the sea.
Þeir voru fimmtán saman.	They were fifteen altogether.	There were fifteen of them together.
Þeir komu um sumarið að jöklinum Hvítserk og höfðu fundið nokkurar eldstóar manna og enn nokkurn veiðiskap.	They came about summer to a-glacier Hvitserk and had-they found some fire-place men and still some hunting.	They came in the summer to the glacier Hvitserk and had found several small groups of men and still some hunting.
Þá mælti Sigurður:	Then spoke Sigurd:	Then Sigurd said:
"Hvors eruð þér fúsari, að hverfa aftur eða fara lengra?	"Which are you willing, to turn back or travel longer?	"Which are you more willing to go back or go further?
Er nú eigi sumars mikið eftir en fang orðið lítið".	Is now not summer much remaining but resources have-become little".	There isn't much left of the summer now, but the catch has become short".
Hásetar kváðust fúsari aftur að hverfa og sögðu mannhættu mikla að fara um stórfjörðu undir jöklum.	The-crew said willing back to turn and said dangerous much to travel about large-fjords under glaciers.	The crew said they were more willing to turn back and said that it was very dangerous to go through a large fjord under glaciers.
Hann kvað það satt "en svo segir mér hugur um að eftir muni hið meira fangið ef því náir".	He said that true "but so says to-me mind about that later would then more to-catch if then getting".	He said it was true "but then my mind tells me that later the more will be caught if it is possible".
Þeir báðu hann ráða, kváðust lengi hans forsjá hlítt hafa og þó vel gefist.	They asked him advice, said long his foresight satisfactory had and though well given.	They asked him for advice, saying that they had been under his guardianship for a long time and that it had been successful.
Honum kveðst meira um að halda fram og svo var gert.	He said more about that to-hold from and so was done.	He said that there was more to claim, and so it was done.
Steinþór hét maður er á skipi þeirra var.	Steinthor was-named a-man was on ship theirs was.	A man on their ship was called Steinthor.
Hann tók til orða:	He took to words:	He spoke:
"Dreymdi mig í nótt Sigurður",	"Dreamed me about the-night Sigurd",	"I had a dream last night, Sigurd",

The Tale of the Greenlanders (II) (The Tale of Einarr Sokkason) (Old Icelandic)

Old Icelandic	Literal	English
sagði hann, "og mun eg segja þér drauminn	said he, "and will I say to-you the-dream	he said, "and I will tell you the dream
nú.	now.	Now
Er vér fórum á fjörðinn þennan hinn mikla þóttist eg kominn í milli bjarga nokkurra og æpa til bjargar mér".	When we travel to fjord then the much thought I coming in between rescuing something and shouting to rescue me".	when we went to this great fjord, I thought I came between something to be rescued from, and shouting for my rescue".
Sigurður kvað draum meðallagi góðan "og skyldir þú þar eigi björg undir fótum troða og hitta eigi í þann einangur að þú mættir eigi munni halda".	Sigurd said dream moderately good "and should you there not rocks under feet tread and find not in that alone-going that you might not mouth hold".	Sigurd said it was a moderately good dream "and you should not trample rocks under your feet there and you should not find yourself so alone that you could not keep your mouth shut".
Steinþór var heldur æðimaður í skaplyndi og óforsjáll.	Steinthor was rather of-mind in temper and impulsive.	Steinthor was rather a hot-tempered and impulsive person.
Og er þeir sækja inn á fjörðinn þá mælti Sigurður:	And when they sought in the fjord then spoke Sigurd:	And when they entered the fjord, Sigurd said:
"Hvort er sem mér sýnist að skip sé inn á fjörðinn?"	"Whether is as to-me seems that ship this in the fjord?"	"Does it seem to me that a ship is in the fjord?"
Þeir kváðu svo vera.	They said so being.	They said it was so.
Sigurður kvað það tíðindum mundu gegna.	Sigurd said that news would pass.	Sigurd said that this would bring great news.
Héldu nú síðan inn að og sáu að skipið var sett upp í einn árós og gert fyrir ofan.	Held now then in to and saw the ship was sat up in a river-mouth and made for above.	Now they went inward and saw that the ship was set up in one estuary and made covered.
Það var mikið hafskip.	It was a-great sea-going-ship.	It was a great sea-going ship.
Síðan gengu þeir á land og sáu skála og tjald skammt frá.	Then went they to land and saw cabin and tent a-short-distance from.	Then they went ashore and saw a cabin and a tent nearby.
Þá mælti Sigurður að þeir mundu tjalda fyrst "og er nú liðið á dag og vil eg að menn séu kyrrrlátir og varúðgir".	Then spoke Sigurd that they would tent-up first "and is now passed in the-day and wish I that men are still and cautious".	Then Sigurd said that they would camp first "and now it's late in the day and I want people to be quiet and careful".
Og svo gerðu þeir.	And so done was.	And so it was done.

The Tale of the Greenlanders (II) (The Tale of Einarr Sokkason) (Old Icelandic)

Old Icelandic	Literal	English
Og um morguninn ganga þeir og sjást um.	And about morning went they and looked about.	And in the morning they went and looked about.
Þeir sjá stokk einn hjá sér og stóð í bol öx og mannshræ hjá.	They saw a-log one beside them and stood in the-trunk an-axe and human-body beside.	They saw a log by them and an axe in the butt and a human carcass.
Sigurður kvað þann mann viðinn höggið hafa og hafa orðið vanmeginn af megri.	Sigurd said that the-man the-trees struck had and had become weak of meagre.	Sigurd said that the man had been striking trees and had become weak from hunger.
Síðan gengu þeir að skálanum og sáu þar annað mannshræ.	Then went they to the-cabin and saw there another dead-body.	Then they walked to the cabin and saw another corpse there.
Sigurður kvað þann gengið hafa meðan hann mátti "og munu þessir verið hafa þjónustumenn þeirra er í skálanum eru".	Sigurd said then walked had as-long-as he might "and would these been have servants-of they who about the-cabin were".	Sigurd said that he had walked for as long as he could "and these will be the servants of who are in the cabin".
Öx lá og hjá þessum.	Axe lay also beside these.	An axe lay beside these.
Þá mælti Sigurður:	Then spoke Sigurd:	Then Sigurd said:
"Það kalla eg ráð að rjúfa skálann og láta leggja út daun af líkum þeim er inni eru og ýldu er lengi mun legið hafa.	"It call I decide to break-open the-hut and lay-out have out the-dead of bodies they who in were and decay are long may laid have.	"This I call our plan, to break open the cabin and let the stench of the dead out, for the corpses will have been lying there for a long time.
Og varist menn fyrir að verða því að þess er eigi lítil von að mönnum verði að því mein og mjög er á mót eðli manna þótt líkindi séu á því að menn þessir muni oss ekki illt gera".	And weariness men for that be because that this is not little hope that men be that because-of disease and much is to meet nature man's though alike they-are that they the men these should to-us not ill be-done".	And men be wary of it, because there is nothing more certain than men will be harmed by it, and it is very against human wellbeing, and though there are similarities, these men will not harm us".
Steinþór kvað slíkt undarlegt að gera sér meira fyrir en þyrfti og gekk á hurðina en þeir rufu skálann.	Steinthor said such strange to do as more for than needed and went to the-door but they broke-up the-cabin.	Steinthor said that it was such a strange thing to do more than was necessary, and went to the door as they broke open the cabin.
Og er Steinþór gekk út þá leit Sigurður til hans og mælti:	And when Steinthor went out then looked Sigurd to him and said:	And when Steinthor came out Sigurd got a look at him and said:

The Tale of the Greenlanders (II) (The Tale of Einarr Sokkason) (Old Icelandic)

Old Icelandic	Literal	English
"Allmjög er manninum brugðið".	"All-great is this-man upset".	"This man is greatly upset".
Hann tók þegar að æpa og hlaupa en þeir eftir félagar hans.	He took straightaway to shouting and running but they followed companions his.	He started shouting and running away, but his companions followed him.
Hann hleypur síðan í hamarrifu nokkura þar er engi mátti að honum komast og þar fékk hann bana.	He ran then into crags some there where no-one might to him come and there got he death.	He ran into some crags and became stuck between them so that no-one could get to him, and there he died.
Sigurður kvað hann of berdreyman.	Sigurd said he of clear-dreams.	Sigurd said his dream was clearly true.
Síðan rufu þeir skálann og gerðu eftir því sem Sigurður mælti og varð þeim ekki mein að.	Then tore-up they the-cabin and did following according as Sigurd said and came to-them not harm by.	Then they tore up the cabin and followed accordingly as Sigurd had told them, and no harm came to them.
Þeir sáu þar í skálanum menn dauða og fé mikið.	They saw there in the-cabin men dead and wealth much.	They saw dead people and a lot of money in the cabin.
Þá mælti Sigurður:	Then said Sigurd:	Then Sigurd said:
"Það sýnist mér ráð að þér hleypið holdi af beinum þeirra í heitukötlum þeirra er þeir hafa átt og er svo hægra til kirkju að færa.	"That seems to-me advisable that you discharge flesh off bones theirs in boiling-cauldrons theirs that they had had and then so right to the-church to bring.	"It seems to me advisable that you get the flesh off their bones in their hot cauldrons that they have, and then move them to church.
Og er það líkast að Arnbjörn muni hér verið hafa því að skip þetta annað hið fagra er hér stendur á landi hefi eg heyrt að hann hafi átt".	And is that likely that Arnbjorn should here been has because that ship this other then the-fairest is here standing about the-land have I heard that he had had".	And it seems likely that Arnbjorn will have been here, because this ship is one of the most beautiful that is standing on this land, I have heard that he had".
Það var höfðaskip og steint og mikil gersemi.	It was a-headed-ship and stone-carving and much treasure.	It was a ship with a figurehead and stone-carving and great treasure.
Kaupskipið var brotið mjög neðan og kvaðst Sigurður ætla að það mundi að engum nytjum verða.	Merchant-ship was broken much below and said Sigurd suppose that it would to no use be.	The merchant ship was broken below, and Sigurd said that it would be of no use.

The Tale of the Greenlanders (II) (The Tale of Einarr Sokkason) (Old Icelandic)

Old Icelandic	Literal	English
Þeir taka úr sauminn en brenndu skipið og höfðu hlaðna ferjuna úr óbyggðum, eftirbátinn og höfðaskipið.	They took out-from the-seam and burned the-ship and had loaded the-ferry out-of the-unsettled-land, the-after-boat and head-ship.	They took out everything from the seams and burned the ship and had loaded to ferry out of the unsettled land, the second boat, and the head ship.
Þeir komu í byggðina og fundu biskup í Görðum og sagði Sigurður honum tíðindin og fjárfundinn.	They came to the-settlement and found bishop in Gardar and said Sigurd to-him the-news and wealth-finding.	They came to the settlement and found the bishop at Gardar, and Sigurd told him the news and of finding the wealth.
"Nú kann eg eigi annað að sjá",	"Now can I not anything-else to see",	"Now I can't see anything else",
sagði hann, "en það fé þeirra muni best komið er beinum þeirra fylgir og ef eg á nokkuru ráð þá vil eg að svo sé".	said he, "but that wealth theirs would best come that bones theirs followed and if I of some advice then wish I to so to-be".	he said, "but their money will be best served if their placed with their bones, and if I have any say, I want it to be so".
Biskup kvað hann vel hafa með farið og viturlega og það mæltu allir.	Bishop said he well had with going and wise-like and that said all.	The bishop said he had acted well and wisely, and everyone said so.
Mikið fé fylgdi líkum þeirra.	Much wealth followed bodies theirs.	A lot of money followed their corpses.
Biskup kvað gersemi mikla vera höfðaskipið.	Bishop said treasure much being head-ship.	The bishop said the great treasure was the head ship.
Sigurður kvað og það sannlegast að það færi til staðarins fyrir sálum þeirra.	Sigurd said and it truthfully that it going to the-place for souls theirs.	Sigurd said, and most truly, that it would go to the bishop's seat for the good of their souls.
Öðru fé skiptu þeir með sér er fundið höfðu að grænlenskum lögum.	Other wealth divided they with themselves as found had to Greenlandic law.	They shared the other money they had found according to Greenlandic law.
Og er þessi tíðindi komu til Noregs þá spurði það sá maður er Össur hét og var systurson Arnbjarnar.	And when these tidings came to Norway then learned that so man was Ossur named and was sister's-son Arnbjarnar.	And when these tidings came to Norway, the man whose name was Ossur, who was Arnbjorn's sister's son, learned about it.
...og	and...	...and
fleiri menn voru þeir á því skipi er sína frændur höfðu misst og væntu til greiðslu um féið.	more men were they in because the-ship was themselves kinsmen had lost and expected to compensation about wealth.	there were more men on the ship that had lost their cousins and were expecting payment for the money.

The Tale of the Greenlanders (II) (The Tale of Einarr Sokkason) (Old Icelandic)

Old Icelandic	Literal	English
Þeir komu í Eiríksfjörð og sóttu menn til fundar við þá og slógu kaupum.	They came to Eriksfjord and sought men to meet with then and strike a-deal.	They came to Eriksfjord and fetched people to meet them and make a deal.
Síðan tóku menn sér vistir.	Then took men themselves supplies.	Then people took supplies.
Össur stýrimaður fór í Garða til biskups og var þar um veturinn.	Ossur steersman went to Gardar to the-bishop and was there about winter.	Ossur the steersman went to Gardar to see the bishop and stayed there during the winter.
Í Vestribyggð var þá annað kaupskip.	In Vestribyggd was then another merchant-ship.	In the Western Settlement there was another merchant ship then.
Þar var Kolbeinn Þorljótsson, norrænn maður.	There was Kolbein Son-of-Thorljot, Nordic man.	There was Kolbein Son-of-Thorljot, a Nordic man.
Hinu þriðja skipi réð sá maður er Hermundur hét og var Koðránsson og Þorgils bróðir hans og höfðu mikla sveit manna.	The third ship commanded so man was Hermund named and was Son-of-Kodran and Thorgils brother his and had much company of-men.	The third ship was commanded by a man named Hermund, who was the son of Kodran, and his brother Thorgils, and they had a large force of men.

3

Um veturinn kom Össur að máli við biskup að hann ætti þangað févon eftir Arnbjörn frænda sinn og beiddi biskup þar gera greiða á bæði fyrir sína hönd og annarra manna.	About winter came Ossur to discuss with the-bishop that he had from-there fee-trust after Arnbjorn kinsman his and bid bishop there to-give assistance as asked for his hand and other men.	During the winter, Ossur discussed with the bishop that he had a trust there for his uncle Arnbjorn and asked the bishop there to give assistance both on his behalf and on other people's behalf.
Biskup kvaðst fé tekið hafa eftir grænlenskum lögum eftir slíka atburði, kvaðst þetta eigi gert hafa með einræði sitt, kvað það maklegast að það fé færi þeim til sáluhjápar er aflað höfðu og til þeirrar kirkju er bein þeirra voru að grafin, sagði það manndómsleysi að kalla nú til fjár þess.	The-bishop said wealth taken had after Greenlandic law after such events, said it not made had with self-will this, said that most that it wealth go-to them to souls who gain had and to their church where bones theirs were to in-the-grave, said that meanness to claim now to money this.	The bishop said that he had taken money according to Greenlandic laws after such events, he said that he had not done this with his decision-making, he said that it was most appropriate that the money should go to the souls they had earned and to the church where their bones were buried, he said it was mean to claim now to this money.

The Tale of the Greenlanders (II) (The Tale of Einarr Sokkason) (Old Icelandic)

Old Icelandic	Literal	English
Síðan vildi Össur eigi vera í Görðum með biskupi og fór til sveitunga sinna og héldu sig svo allir samt um veturinn.	Then willed Ossur not to-be at Gardar with the-bishop and went to men-company his and held him so all the-same about winter.	After that, Ossur did not want to stay in Gardar with the bishop and went to his companions, and they all stayed the winter anyway.
Um vorið bjó Össur mál til þings þeirra Grænlendinga og var það þing í Görðum.	About spring prepared Ossur a-case to the-assembly theirs Greenlanders and was it assembly in Gardar.	In the spring, Ossur prepared a case for the assembly of the Greenlanders, and that meeting was held in Gardar.
Kom þar biskup og Einar Sokkason og höfðu þeir fjölmenni mikið.	Came there bishop and Einar Son-of-Sokki and had they following-men many.	Bishop and Einar Sokkason came there and they had a lot of followers.
Össur kom þar og skipverjar hans.	Ossur came there and crew his.	Ossur and his crew arrived there.
Og er dómur var settur þá gekk Einar að dómi með fjölmenni og kveðst ætla að þeim mundi erfitt að eiga við útlenda menn í Noregi ef svo skyldi þar.	And when judgement was set then went Einar to the-court with many-people and said supposed to them would difficult to have with foreign men in Norway if so should there.	And when the sentence was passed, Einar went to the court with many people and said that they would find it difficult to deal with foreigners in Norway if it happened there.
"Viljum vér þau lög hafa er hér ganga",	"Wish we then law have that here going",	"We wish to have the law that goes here",
sagði Einar.	said Einar.	said Einar.
Og er dómurinn fór út náðu Austmenn eigi málum fram að koma og stukku frá.	And when the-judgement went out reached Eastern-men not case from to come and went-away from.	And when the judgement came out, the Eastern-men could not progress forward and went away.
Nú líkar Össuri illa, þykist hafa af óvirðing en fé ekki og varð það hans úrræði að hann fer til þar er skipið er það hið steinda og hjó úr tvö borð, sínu megin hvort upp frá kilinum.	Now likes Ossur ill, seems have of un-worthy but wealth not and became it his solution that he went to there where the-ship was that the stone-one and struck out-of two boards, theirs sides each up from the-keel.	Now Ossur did not like this and thought ill of it, because of the disrespect not the money, and so became his solution, that he went to where the ship was that had the stone and struck out two boards, one on each side, upwards from the keel.
Eftir það fór hann til Vestribyggðar og hitti þá Kolbein og Ketil Kálfsson og sagði þeim svo búið.	After that went he to Vestribygd and met then Kolbein and Ketil Son-of-Kalf and said to-them so settled.	After that he went to Vestribyggd (The-Western-Settlement) and met Kolbein and Ketil Kalfsson and told them it was over.

The Tale of the Greenlanders (II) (The Tale of Einarr Sokkason) (Old Icelandic)

Old Icelandic	Literal	English
Kolbeinn kvað ósæmd til tekna enda sagði hann úrræðið eigi gott.	Kolbein said dishonourable to taken and said he solution not good.	Kolbein said that it was taken as dishonourable and that the solution was not good.
Ketill mælti:	Ketil said:	Ketil said:
"Fýsa vil eg þig að þú ráðist hingað til vor því að eg hefi spurt fastmæli biskups og Einars en þú munt vanfær að sitja fyrir tilstilli biskups en framkvæmd Einars og verum heldur allir saman".	"Desire will I you that you advise here until spring because that I have learned opinion the-bishop's and Einar's but you would unable to sit through guidance the-bishop's but execution Einar's and we rather all together".	"I want you to come here until spring, because I have learned the bishop's and Einar's opinion, and you will be unable to sit through the bishop's guidance, and Einar's actions and we should rather all stand together".
Hann kvað það og líklegast að það mundi af ráðast.	He said that and likely that it would of be-arranged.	He said that it was so, and it would likely be arranged.
Þar var í sveit með þeim kaupmönnum Ísa-Steingrímur.	There was in the-company with them trading-men Isa-Steingrim.	There was in the company of merchants with them a man named Isa-Steingrim.
Össur fór þá aftur til Kiðjabergs.	Ossur went then back to Kidjaberg.	Ossur then went back to Kidjaberg.
Þar hafði hann áður verið.	There had he before been.	He had been there before.

4

Biskup varð reiður mjög er hann spurði að spillt var skipinu og kallar til sín Einar Sokkason og mælti:	Bishop became angry much when he learned that damaged was the-ship and called to him Einar Son-of-Sokki and said:	The Bishop became very-much angry when he learned of the damage that was done to the ship, and called Einar Sokkason before him and said:
"Nú er til þess að taka er þú hést með svardaga er vér fórum af Noregi að refsa svívirðing staðarins og hans eigna við þá er það gerðu.	"Now it to this that take what you promised with oath was we travelled from Norway to punish disgrace of-the-place and its property with then is it to-do.	"Now it is for you to take action as you promised by oath when we travelled from Norway, to punish the disgrace to this place and its property and those who did it.
Nú kalla eg Össur hafa fyrirgert sér er hann hefir spillt eign vorri og sýnt oss í öllum hlutum óþekktarsvip.	Now call I Ossur have before-done himself as he has damaged property ours and shown us to ill things ungraceful.	Now I announce that Ossur's life is forfeit, as he has damaged our property and shown us the most disgraceful ill.

The Tale of the Greenlanders (II) (The Tale of Einarr Sokkason) (Old Icelandic)

Old Icelandic	Literal	English
Nú er ekki að dyljast við að mér líkar eigi svo búið og eg kalla þig eiðrofa ef kyrrt er".	Now is none to hiding with that to-me like not so settled and I call you breach-of-oath if still are".	Now there is no hiding that I do not like things as they so are, and I will call you in breach of oath if they still are".
Einar svarar:	Einar answered:	Einar answered:
"Eigi er þetta vel gert herra en mæla munu það sumir að nokkur vorkunn sé á við Össur, svo miklu sem hann er sviptur, þótt eigi sé vel í höndum haft þá er þeir sáu góða gripi er frændur þeirra höfðu átt og náðu eigi.	"Not is this well done sir but badly would that some that some pity is to with Ossur, so much as he is deprived, though not is well in handling has then is they saw good treasure that kinsmen theirs had owned and reached not.	"This is not a good thing to have done sir, but it would be bad for some may pity Ossur, for he has been deprived of so much, and it will not be handled well if they saw the good treasure that their kinsmen had owned and were unable to obtain it.
Og veit eg varla hverju eg skal hér um heita".	And knowing I hardly how I shall here about be-called".	And I hardly know how I shall call this.
Þeir skildu fálega og var reiðisvipur á biskupi.	They parted coolly and was angry of the-bishop.	They parted coolly, and the bishop looked angry.
Og þá er menn sóttu til kirkjumessu og til veislu á Langanes var biskup þar og Einar að veislunni.	And then when men sought to church-mass and to feast at Langanes was the-bishop there and Einar at the-feast.	And when people went to church mass and to a feast at Langanes, the bishop was there and Einar was at the feast.
Margt fólk var komið til tíða og söng biskup messu.	Many folk were come to the-service and sang the-bishop mass.	Many people had come and the bishop sang mass.
Þar var kominn Össur og stóð undir kirkju sunnan og við kirkjuvegginn og talaði sá maður við hann er Brandur hét og var Þórðarson, heimamaður biskups.	There was come Ossur and standing under the-church to-the-south and with church-wall and told so man with him was Brand named and was Son-of-Thord, house-man the-bishop's.	Ossur had arrived there and was standing under the church to the south and by the church wall, and talking to the man with him whose name was Brand Thorisson, the bishop's houseman.
Þessi maður bað Össur vægja til við biskup "og vænti eg",	This man bid Ossur make-peace to with the-bishop "and expect I",	This man asked Ossur to make peace with the bishop, "and I expect",
sagði hann, "að þá muni vel duga en nú agir við svo".	said he, "that then would well aided but not desirable with so".	he said, "that all will be well, but it is not desirable as it is".
Össur kvaðst ekki fá það af sér svo illa sem við hann var búið.	Ossur said not get that of him so ill as with he was settled.	Ossur said that he could not because of the ill with which it had been concluded.

The Tale of the Greenlanders (II) (The Tale of Einarr Sokkason) (Old Icelandic)

Old Icelandic	Literal	English
Og áttu þeir nú um þetta að tala.	And have they now about this to spoke.	And they now spoke about this.
Þá gengu þeir biskup frá kirkju og heim til húsa og var Einar þar í göngu.	Then went they the-bishop from the-church and home to house and was Einar there in going.	Then the bishop and the others went from the church to the house, and Einar went along.
Og er þeir komu fyrir skáladyrnar þá snerist Einar frá fylgdinni og gekk einn í brott til kirkjugarðsins og tók öxi úr hendi tíðamanni einum og gekk suður um kirkjuna.	And as they came before the-door then turned Einar from following and went alone to away to churchyard and took axe out-of hand worshippers one and went south around the-church.	And as they came to the door then Einar turned away from the followers and went away alone to the churchyard and took an axe out of the hand of one of the worshippers and went around to the south side of the church.
Össur stóð þar og studdist á öxi sína.	Ossur stood there and stood on axe his.	Ossur stood there leaning on his axe.
Einar hjó hann þegar banahögg og gekk inn eftir það og voru þá borð uppi.	Einar struck him straight-away death-blow and went in after that and were then the-tables up.	Einar struck him a death blow straight away and went inside by which time the tables were up.
Einar steig undir borðið gegnt biskupi og mælti ekki orð.	Einar stepped under the-table opposite the-bishop and spoke not a-word.	Einar took his seat at the table opposite the bishop and spoke not a word.
Síðan gekk hann Brandur Þórðarson í stofuna og fyrir biskup og mælti:	Then went he Brand Son-of-Thord in sitting-room and before bishop and said:	Then Brand Thordarson went into the sitting room before the bishop and said:
"Er nokkuð tíðinda sagt yður herra?"	"Is some news told you sir?"	"Has some news been told to you sir?"
Biskup kvaðst eigi spurt hafa "eða hvað segir þú?"	Bishop said not learned had "but what say you?"	The bishop said he had not heard "but what say you?"
Hann svarar:	He answered:	He answered:
"Sígast lét nú einn hér úti".	"Sinking laid now one here outside".	"Someone has dropped down laying dead here outside".
Biskup mælti:	Bishop spoke:	The bishop said:
"Hver veldur því eða hver er fyrir orðinn?"	"Who caused therefore or who is before the-words?"	"Who causes it or who is behind the word?"

The Tale of the Greenlanders (II) (The Tale of Einarr Sokkason) (Old Icelandic)

Old Icelandic	Literal	English
Brandur kvað þann nær er frá kunni að segja.	Brand said then as-far as from known to say.	Brand said someone as far away as him knew to say.
Biskup mælti:	Bishop said:	The bishop said:
"Veldur þú Einar líftjóni Össurar?"	"Brought-about you Einar loss-of-life Ossur?"	"Did you bring about Ossur's loss of life, Einar?"
Hann svarar:	He answered:	He answered:
"Því veld eg víst".	"Because willed I certainly".	"This I willed certainly".
Biskup mælti:	The-bishop said:	The bishop said:
"Eigi eru slík verk góð en þó er vorkunn á".	"Not are-they such work good but though is pity about".	"Such work is not good, but there is pity about it".
Brandur bað að þvo skyldi líkinu og syngja yfir.	Brand bid that washed should the-body and sung over.	Brand asked that the body should be washed and a service sung over.
Biskup kvað mundu gefa tóm til þess	Bishop said would give time to this	The bishop said that there would be time to give to this,
og sátu menn undir borðum og fóru að öllu tómlega og fékk biskup svo fremi menn til að syngja yfir líkinu en Einar bað þess og kvað það sama að gera það með sæmd.	and sat people under the-tables and went to all time-like and went bishop so provided men to that sing over the-body as Einar bid this and said that same that to-do that with honour.	and the people sat at the tables taking their time, and so it went that the bishop provided men to sing over the body as Einar had asked, saying that it should be done with some honour.
Biskuð kvaðst ætla að það mun réttara að grafa hann eigi að kirkju "en þó við bæn þína skal hann hér jarða að þessi kirkju að eigi er heimilisprestur".	The-bishop said supposed to that would more-correct to grave him not at church "but though with bidding yours shall he here earthed to this church that not with local-priest".	The bishop supposed that it would be more correct not to bury him at a church "but because of your asking, he shall be buried at this church that does not have a resident priest".
Og fékk hann eigi til fyrr kennimenn yfir að syngja en áður var um lík búið.	And got he not to for priests over to sing but after was about the-body prepared.	And he did not get priests to sing over him as his body was being prepared.
Þá mælti Einar:	Then said Einar:	Then Einar said:

The Tale of the Greenlanders (II) (The Tale of Einarr Sokkason) (Old Icelandic)

Old Icelandic	Literal	English
"Nú hefir orðið í stökki brang og ekki lítt af yðru tilstilli en hér eiga þó hlut í ofsamenn miklir og get eg að stórir úfar rísi á með oss".	"Now has-been become in blood-splattered chest and not little of your agency but here not though part in overbearing-men much and get I that badly misfortune giants of with us".	"Now there has become bloodshed, in no small amount by your doing, and here are very powerful men, and I can tell that a great misfortune will be with us".
Biskup kvaðst vænta að menn munu þessum ofsa af sér hrinda en unna sæmdar fyrir mál þetta og umdæmis ef eigi væri með ofsa að gengið.	The-bishop said hoped that people would this violence of themselves repel but win honour for matter this and area if not was with violence of going.	The bishop said that he hoped that the people who would bring this violence would be repelled, and that they would win honour in this matter as long as there was no violence.

5

Old Icelandic	Literal	English
Tíðindi þessi spurðust og fréttu það kaupmenn.	News this heard-of and found-out the trading-men.	News of this was heard of, and it was found out among the merchants.
Þá mælti Ketill Kálfsson:	Then said Ketil Son-of-Kalf:	Then Ketil Kalfsson said:
"Ekki fór fjarri getu minni að honum mundi höfuðgjarnt verða".	"Not for far ability mine that he would headstrong be".	"It is not outside of my ability if he would be headstrong".
Maður hét Símon, frændi Össurar, mikill maður og sterkur.	Man was-named Simon, kinsman Ossur, great man and strong.	There was a man named Simon, a kinsman of Ossur, a great and strong man.
Ketill kvað vera mega ef Símon fylgdi atgervi sinni "að hann mun muna dráp Össurar frænda síns".	Ketil said to-be may of Simon follow plan his "that he would remember killing Of-Ossur kinsman his".	Ketil said that if Simon followed his plan "that he would remember the killing of his kinsman Ossur".
Símon kvaðst þar eigi mundu ferleg orð um hafa.	Simon said that not would-be fair words about had.	Simon said that there would be no good words to be had about it.
Ketill lét búa skip þeirra og sendi menn á fund Kolbeins stýrimanns og sagði honum tíðindin "og segið honum svo að eg skal fara með máli á hendur Einari því mér eru kunnig grænlensk lög og er eg búinn til við þá.	Ketil had prepared ship theirs and sent men to meet Kolbein steersman and said to-him the-news "and say to-him so that I shall travel with the-matter in hand Einar because to-me they-are known Greenlandic laws and that I prepared to with them.	Ketil had prepared their ship and sent men to meet Kolbein the steersman and tell him the news "and say to him that I will prosecute Einar for the matter in hand, because the Greenlandic laws are known to me, and I am prepared to deal with them.

The Tale of the Greenlanders (II) (The Tale of Einarr Sokkason) (Old Icelandic)

Old Icelandic	Literal	English
Höfum vér og mikinn liðskost ef að oss kemst".	Have we-are and much force of to us come".	We have a great advantage of company if it comes to us".
Símon kvaðst vilja Ketils ráðum fram fara.	Simon said wished-for Ketil's advice from going.	Simon said that he wished for Ketil's advice going forward.
Síðan fór hann og hitti Kolbein, sagði honum vígið og þar með orðsending Ketils og þeir skyldu snúast til liðveislu við þá úr Vestribyggð og sækja til þings þeirra Grænlendinga.	Then went he and found Kolbein, said to-him killing and there with word-sending Ketil's and they should return to support with then out-of Vestribyggd and seek to assembly theirs Greenland.	Then he went and found Kolbein, and told him of the killing, and that they should return to support them at Vestribyggd and attend the Greenland assembly.
Kolbeinn kvaðst koma mundu að vissu ef hann mætti og kvaðst vilja að Grænlendingum yrði það eigi hagkeypi að drepa menn þeirra.	Kolbein said come would to know if he might and said willed to Greenland become that not good-bargain that killing men theirs.	Kolbein said that they would certainly come if he did and said that he wanted the Greenlanders to not have to kill their men.
Ketill tók þegar mál af Símoni og fór með nokkura sveit manna en sagði að þeir kaupmenn skyldu halda skjótt eftir "og hafið varning með yður".	Ketil took them the-matter of Simon and went with some company men but said that they trading-men should rather away afterwards "and have wares with you".	Ketil immediately took the matter with Simon and went with a few men, but said that the merchants should leave quickly "and take your goods with you".
Kolbeinn fór þegar er honum komu þessi orð, bað og félaga sína fara til þings og kveðst þá hafa svo mikla sveit að óvíst væri að Grænlendingar sætu yfir hlut þeirra.	Kolbein went straightaway when he came these words, asked and companions his went to the-assembly and said then had so much company that uncertain was that Greenlanders reconcile over lot theirs.	Kolbein left as soon as these words came to him, and asked his companions to go to the assembly and declared that they had such a large force that it was uncertain that the Greenlanders would be able to handle their lot.
Nú hittust þeir Kolbeinn og Ketill og báru ráð sín saman.	Now found they Kolbein and Ketil and carried advice theirs together.	Now they met Kolbein and Ketil and discussed their advice.
Hvortveggji þeirra var gildur maður.	Each of-them was valid man.	Each of them was a valid man.
Nú fóru þeir og bægði þeim veður og komast þó fram og höfðu mikla sveit manna en þó minni en þeir hugðu.	Now travelled they and prevented them weather and came though from and they-had large company of-men but though less than they thought.	Now they travelled and the weather prevented them but they came through it, and they had a large company of men but less than they thought.

The Tale of the Greenlanders (II) (The Tale of Einarr Sokkason) (Old Icelandic)

Old Icelandic	Literal	English
Nú komu menn til þings.	Now came men to the-assembly.	Now the men came to the assembly.
Sokki var þar kominn Þórisson.	Sokki was there coming Son-of-Thorri.	Sokki Thorisson came there too.
Hann var vitur maður og var þá gamall og mjög tekinn til að gera um mál manna.	He was wise man and was then old and very taken to that doing about matters peoples'.	He was a wise man and was very old by then, and was often taken to dealing with peoples' matters.
Hann gengur á fund þeirra Kolbeins og Ketils og kvaðst vilja leita um sættir.	He went to meet them Kolbein and Ketil and said willed seek about reconciliation.	He went to meet Kolbein and Ketil and said that he wished to seek reconciliation.
"Vil eg bjóðast til",	"Will I offer to",	"I wish to offer",
segir hann, "að gera í milli yðvar.	said he, "to make in between you.	he said, "to make this between you.
Og þótt mér sé meiri vandi á við Einar son minn þá skal það þó um gera er mér og öðrum vitrum mönnum líst nær sanni".	And though I him more custom to with Einar son mine then shall it though about be-done that I and others wise men behold nearer the-truth".	And even though I have a bigger custom with Einar my son, it will still be about what I and other wise men think is closer to the truth".
Ketill kvaðst ætla að þeir mundu málum fram halda til málsfyllingar en fyrirkveðast eigi að taka sættir "en þó er ört að gengið við oss en höfum ekki vanist því hér til að minnka vorn hlut".	Ketil said intended that they would the-matter from hold until the-matter-fulfilling but refusing not to take reconciliation "but though we-are swiftly to going with us but have not custom as here to of decreased our lot".	Ketil said that they intended to take the matter to its conclusion, and refused to rule out a reconciliation "and though we are being treated swiftly, we are not accustomed to reducing our share".
Sokki kveðst ætla að þeir munu eigi jafnt að vígi standa og kvað óvíst að þeir fengju meiri sæmd þó hann dæmdi eigi.	Sokki said supposed that they would not equal to battle stand and said uncertain that they would-get more honour though he judged not.	Sokki said he supposed that they won't be equal if it came to a battle, and said it was uncertain that they would get any more honour though he would not judge the matter.
Kaupmenn gengu að dómi og hafði Ketill mál frammi á hönd Einari.	The-merchants went to court and had Ketil the-case from in hand Einar.	The merchants went to court and Ketil had the case in hand from Einar.
Það mælti Einar:	This said Einar:	Then Einar said:
"Það mun víða spyrjast ef þeir bera oss hér málum"	"It will-be widely known-about if they bear us here cases"	"It will be widely known about if they bear this case here"

The Tale of the Greenlanders (II) (The Tale of Einarr Sokkason) (Old Icelandic)

Old Icelandic	Literal	English
og gekk að dóminum og hleypir upp og fengu þeir eigi haldið.	and went to the-court and released up and got they not holding.	and went into the court and broke it up and they did not get their proceedings.
Þá mælti Sokki:	Then said Sokki:	Then Sokki said:
"Kostur skal enn þess er eg bauð, að sættast og geri eg um málið".	"Choice shall one this that I asked-for, to reconcile and make I about the-case".	"The choice shall be one that I asked for to reconcile, and I shall make the case".
Ketill kvaðst ætla að það mundi nú ekki verða "er þú leggur til yfirbóta það er þó er hinn sami ójafnaður Einars um þetta mál"	Ketil said intended that it would now not be "but you propose to over-compensation it that though is the same unequal Einar about that case"	Ketil said that he supposed that it would now not be "but to propose more compensation would be just as unequal to Einar in the case"
og skildu að því.	and separated to accordingly.	and they separated accordingly.
En því komu kaupmenn eigi úr Vestribyggð til þings að þá var andviðri er þeir voru búnir með tveim skipum.	But then came the-merchants alone from Vestribyggd to the-assembly that then were the-storm that they were prepared with two ships.	But then came the merchants from Vestribyggd to the assembly that were in the storm and prepared with two ships.
En að miðju sumri skyldi sætt gera á Eiði.	But in the-middle of-summer should settled be in Eid.	But in the middle of summer a settlement should be made at Eid.
Þá komu þeir kaupmenn vestan og lögðu að við nes nokkuð og hittust þeir þá allir saman og áttu stefnur.	Then came they the-trading-men western and laid at with headland some and met they then all together and had plans.	Then the merchants came from the west and laid at a certain headland, and they all met up and made their plans.
Þá mælti Kolbeinn að eigi skyldi svo nær hafa gengið um sættirnar ef þeir hefðu allir samt verið "en það þykir mér nú ráð að vér förum allir til þessa fundar með slíkum föngum sem til eru".	Then said Kolbein that not should so close have been about reconciliation if they had all together been "but it seems to-me now advisable that we go all to this meeting with such resources as to they-are".	Then Kolbein said that it should not have been so close to a reconciliation if they had all been together "but it seems to me now advisable that we all go to this meeting with such resources as they are".
Og svo var að þeir fóru og leyndust í leynivogi einum skammt frá biskupsstólnum.	And so was it they went and innermost in hidden-creek one a-short-distance from the-bishop's-seat.	And so it was that they went to the innermost of a certain hidden creek a short distance from the bishop's seat.

The Tale of the Greenlanders (II) (The Tale of Einarr Sokkason) (Old Icelandic)

Old Icelandic	Literal	English
Það bar saman að biskupsstólinum, að hringdi til hámessu og það að Einar Sokkason kom.	It bore together that the-bishop's-seat, that called to high-mass and it that Einar Son-of-Sokki came.	And so it came together that the bishop's seat called a high mass, and Einar Sokkason arrived.
Og er kaupmennirnir heyrðu þetta þá sögðu þeir að mikla skyldi gera virðing til Einars að hringja skal í mót honum og kváðu slík mikil endemi og urðu illa við.	And when the-trading-men heard that then said they that great should be-done worthiness to Einar to call shall in meeting him and saying such great unheard-of and became angry with.	And when the merchants heard that they said that it was paying a great honour to Einar to meet him in such a way, saying that it was a great unheard of, and they became angry with.
Kolbeinn mælti:	Kolbein said:	Kolbein said:
"Verðið eigi illa við þetta því að svo mætti að berast að þetta yrði að líkhringingu áður kveld kæmi".	"Become not ill with this because that so might that bear that this would to funeral-procession before night comes".	"Do not become ill with this, because it might come to be that this will be a funeral procession before night comes".
Nú komu þeir Einar og settust niður í brekku einni.	Now came they Einar and sat down in the-slope alone.	Now came Einar and his men and sat down alone.
Sokki lét fram gripi til virðingar og þá er til gjalds voru ætlaðir.	Sokki laid-out from treasure to worthiness and then when the payment was intended.	Sokki laid out treasures of value that were intended for payment.
Ketill mælti:	Ketil said:	Ketil said:
"Það vil eg að við Hermundur Koðránsson virðum gripina".	"That will I that with Hermund Son-of-Kodran worthiness treasure".	"I wish for Hermund Kodransson and I to value these treasures".
Sokki kvað svo vera skyldu.	Sokki said so being would.	Sokki said that it would be so.
Símon frændi Össurar sýndi á sér ópekktarsvip og reikaði hjá meðan gripagjaldið var sett.	Simon kinsman Of-Ossur showed of himself dishonourable and wandered by while the-artefact-fee was set.	Simon, a kinsman of Ossur, showed himself to be dishonourable and wandered by while the artefacts were being set.
Síðan var fram borin spangabrynja ein forn.	Then was from brought plate-mail one of-old.	Then an ancient plate mal was brought out.
Símon mælti þá:	Simon said then:	Then Simon said:
"Svívirðlega er slíkt boðið fyrir slíkan mann sem Össur var"	"Disgracefully is such offering for such man as Ossur was"	"Such an offering is disgraceful for such a man as Ossur was"

The Tale of the Greenlanders (II) (The Tale of Einarr Sokkason) (Old Icelandic)

Old Icelandic	Literal	English
og kastaði brynjunni á völlinn á burt og gekk upp að þeim er þeir sátu í brekkunni.	and cast the-armour on the-field and way and went up to them as they sat on the-slope.	and he threw the armour away on the field and went up to them as they sat on the slope.
Og er það sáu þeir Grænlendingar þá spretta þeir upp og horfðu forbrekkis og í móti honum Símoni.	And when that saw they Greenlanders then sprang they up and looked downhill and in facing him Simon.	And when the Greenlanders saw that, they sprang up and looked downhill at Simon and faced towards him.
Og því næst gekk Kolbeinn upp hjá þeim er þeir horfðu allir frá og slæst á bak þeim og fór einn frá sínum mönnum.	And then next went Kolbein up beside them when they looked all away-from and slipped in back of-them and went alone from his men.	And then Kolbein went up beside them whey they all looked away and slipped behind them alone from his men.
Og var það jafnsnemma að hann komst á bak Einari og hjó með öxi milli herða honum og Einars öx kom í höfuð Símoni og fengu báðir banasár.	And was it equally-early that he came to back Einar and struck with an-axe between shoulders his and Einar's axe came in head Simon's and got both death-wounds.	And it was just as soon that he got behind Einar and cut him with an axe between his shoulders, and Einar's axe hit Simon in the head and both received mortal wounds.
Einar mælti er hann féll:	Einar said when he fell:	Einar said when he fell:
"Slíks var að von".	"Such was it expected".	"It was so as I expected".
Síðan hljóp Þórður fóstbróðir Einars að Kolbeini og vildi höggva hann en Kolbeinn snaraðist við honum og stakk fram öxarhyrnunni og kom í barkann Þórði og hafði hann þegar bana.	Then ran Thord foster-brother Einar's to Kolbein and wanted to-strike him but Kolbein caught-up with him and thrust from axe-horn and came in throat Thord's and had he instantly killed.	Then Thord, Einar's foster brother, ran to Kolbein and wanted to cut him down, but Kolbein caught up with him and stuck out the axe horn and hit Thord in the throat, killing him instantly.
Síðan slær í bardaga með þeim.	Then struck to battle with them.	Then a battle was struck between them.
Biskup sat hjá Einari og andaðist hann í knjám honum.	Bishop sat beside Einar and died he in knees his.	The bishop sat beside Einar and he died in his lap.
Steingrímur hét maður er það mælti að þeir skyldu gera svo vel að berjast eigi og gekk á milli með nokkura menn en hvorirtveggju voru svo óðir að Steingrímur var lagður sverði í gegnum í þessi hríð.	Steingrim was-named a-man who this said that they should do so well to fight not and went in between with some men but either-side were so angry that Steingrim was laid to-the-sword in through in this time.	There was a man named Steingrim who said that they would do well not to fight and went in between some of the men, but either side was so angry that Steingrim was laid to the sword through him in this time.

The Tale of the Greenlanders (II) (The Tale of Einarr Sokkason) (Old Icelandic)

Old Icelandic	Literal	English
Einar andaðist uppi á brekkunni við búð Grænlendinga.	Einar died up on the-slope by booth The-Greenlanders'.	Einar died up on the slope by the Greenlanders' booth.
Og nú urðu menn sárir mjög og komust þeir Kolbeinn til skips með þrjá sína menn vegna og fóru síðan yfir Einarsfjörð til Skjálgsbúða.	And now became men wounded much and came they Kolbein to ships with three their men slain and went then over Einarsfjord to Skjalgsbud.	And now men became much wounded and Kolbein and his men came to their ships with three men killed and went over to Einarsfjord to Skjalgsbud.
Þar voru kaupskipin og voru þá mjög í búnaði.	There were merchant-ships and were then much in preparations.	The merchant ships were there and they were very much prepared.
Kolbeinn kvað í hafa gerst nokkura róstu "og vil eg ætla að Grænlendingar uni nú eigi betur við en áður".	Kolbein said that had done some uproar "and will I suppose that Greenlanders like now not better with than before".	Kolbein said that there had been some uproar "and I would like to say that the Greenlanders are now no better pleased than before".
Ketill mælti:	Ketil said:	Ketil said:
"Sannyrði gafst þér Kolbeinn",	"True-words gave to-you Kolbein",	"You gave true words Kolbein",
sagði hann, "að vér mundum heyra líkhringinguna áður vér færum í burt og ætla eg að hann Einar sé dauður borinn til kirkju".	said he, "that we would hear the-funeral-procession before we travel to away and suppose I that he Einar is dead carried to the-church".	he said, "that we would hear the funeral procession before we travel away and I suppose that Einar who is dead will be carried to the church".
Kolbeinn kvaðst heldur þannig hafa að stutt.	Kolbein said rather that-way had it supported.	Kolbein said that it was rather that way, that he had supported it.
Ketill mælti:	Ketil said:	Ketil said:
"Þess er von að Grænlendingar muni sækja á vorn fund og kalla eg ráð að menn haldi á búnaði sínum eftir föngum og séu allir á skipum um nætur".	"This is expect that The-Greenlanders will seek to ours meet and call I advice that men hold of equipment theirs after resources and are all to ships about night".	"It is expected that the Greenlanders will seek to meet us, and I advise that the men take hold of their equipment and resources and all stay on the ships overnight".
Og svo gerðu þeir.	And so did they.	And so they did.
Sokki harmaði mjög þessi tíðindi og bað menn fulltingis að veita sér vígsgengi.	Sokki harmed much this news and asked men assistance to grant him in-battle.	Sokki was much harmed by this news and asked the men to grant him assistance in battle.

The Tale of the Greenlanders (II) (The Tale of Einarr Sokkason) (Old Icelandic)

Old Icelandic	Literal	English

6

Hallur hét maður.

Hann bjó að Sólarfjöllum, vitur maður og góður bóndi.

Hann var í liði með Sokka og kom síðast með sínu liði.

Hann mælti til Sokka:

"Ekki vænleg líst mér þín ætlan að leggja smáskipum að stórskipum við slíkan viðbúnað sem eg hygg að þeir munu hafa.

En eg veit eigi hversu traust lið er þú hefir en allir vaskir menn munu vel gefast en hinir munu hlífast meir, og verða höfuðsmenn fyrir það uppgefnir og horfir þá enn þunglegar vor málahlutur en áður.

Nú sýnist mér ráð ef menn skulu að leggja að eiðar fari fram að hver maður skuli annaðhvort hér falla eða hafa sigur".

En við þessu orð Halls dignuðu menn mjög.

Sokki mælti:

"Eigi munum vér þó skilja við þetta, að ósett sé málunum".

Hallur kvaðst mundu leita um sættir milli þeirra og kallaði á kaupmenn og mælti:

6

Hall was-named man.

He lived at Solarfjoll, wise man and good farmer.

He was in company with Sokki and came last with his team.

He said to Sokki:

"Not hopeful behold I your intention to lay small-ships to large-ships with such preparation as I think that they shall have.

But I know not how-so trust team is you have but all brave men should well give but others should protect more, and become head-men for that up-given and where then but the-more-difficult our matter-lot than before.

Now seems to-me advisable if men shall to allow that oath go from to each man shall other-either here fall or have victory".

But with this word Hall's pride lessened much.

Sokki said:

"Not shall we though part with this, that unsettled is the-matter".

Hall said should seek about reconciliation between them and called the trading-men and spoke:

6

There was a man named Hall.

He lived at Solarfjoll, he was a wise man and a good farmer.

He was in company with Sokki and was the last to come to his team.

He said to Sokki:

"I am not hopeful of your intention to lay small ships against large ships with such preparations as I think they will have.

But I don't know how strong a team you have, but all the good men will give well, but the others will be more careful, and the leaders will be exhausted because of it, and then our affairs will be even more difficult than before.

Now it seems to me that if men are to make an oath, each man shall either fall here or be victorious".

But at this word of Hall's, peoples' pride lessened much.

Sokki said:

"However, we will not part with this, that things are not settled".

Hall said that they should seek reconciliation between them and called the merchants and spoke:

The Tale of the Greenlanders (II) (The Tale of Einarr Sokkason) (Old Icelandic)

Old Icelandic	Literal	English
"Hvort skal mér fritt að ganga á fund yðvarn?"	"Whether shall I peace to go to meet with-you?"	"Should I be at peace to go to a meeting with you?"
Þeir Kolbeinn og Ketill svara að honum skyldi fritt.	They Kolbein and Ketil answered that to-him should-be peace.	Kolbein and his men answered that he should be at peace.
Síðan hitti hann þá og lét nauðsyn að málum væri sett eftir slík stórvirki.	Then met he then and had necessary to matter should-be settled after such great-works.	Then he met them and made it necessary that matters should be settled after such great deeds.
Þeir kváðust nú búnir við hvoru sem aðrir vildu, kváðu af þeim landsmönnum allan þennan ójafnað staðið hafa "en nú er þú sýnir svo mikla góðgirnd þá unum vér því að þú gerir í milli vor".	They said now prepared with each as other willed, saying of them lands-men all then unequal stood have "but now are you showed so much good-will then among us therefore that you make to between us".	They said they were ready to do whatever others wanted, they said of those countrymen who have been through this uneven situation "but now you are showing so much kindness, we hope that you do among us".
Hann kvaðst eftir því gera mundu og dæma er honum sýndist réttlegast hversu sem hvorum líkaði.	He said after therefore be-done should and deemed that to-him seemed correctness how-so as each liked.	He said that he would do what he thought was the right thing to do, however everyone liked it.
Síðan var þetta fyrir Sokka borið.	Then was that for Sokki borne.	Then this was put before Sokki.
Hann kveðst og mundu una umdæmi Halls.	He said and would content about-judgement Hall's.	He said that he would be content with Hall's judgement about it.
Kaupmenn skyldu um nætur að búnaði sínum vera og kváðu Sokka ekki annað líka en þeir yrðu í burtu sem fyrst "en ef þeir seinka búnað sinn og gera mér skapraun í því þá er vís von að þeir skulu bótalausir ef þeir verða teknir".	The-trading-men should about the-night to equipment theirs be and said Sokki not other like but they be to away as first "but if they delay preparations theirs and make to-me temperament in because then be aware hope that they shall boat-lose if they become taken".	The merchants had to make their preparations through the night and Sokki said that there was no other way except that they were to be away as soon as possible "but if they delay in their preparations and make to my temperament, then they shall lose their boat if they become taken".
Nú skildu þeir að því og var á sáttarfund kveðið.	Now separated they that accordingly and were in peace-meeting declared.	Now they separated accordingly and a reconciliation meeting was declared.
Ketill mælti:	Ketil said:	Ketil said:

The Tale of the Greenlanders (II) (The Tale of Einarr Sokkason) (Old Icelandic)

Old Icelandic	Literal	English
"Ekki horfir skjótlega búnaður vor en vistföng þverra heldur og er það mitt ráð að leita eftir vistunum og veit eg hvar sá maður býr er mikinn mat á og kalla eg ráð að sækja eftir".	"Not looks shortly equipment ours but resources running-out rather and is it my advice to seek after provisions and know I where so man prepared is much food to and call I advice to seek after".	"It does not look like our equipment will be prepared shortly, and resources are running out, and it is my advice to seek provisions, and I know where there is a man who has much food, and I advise we seek him out".
Þeir kváðust þess albúnir.	They said this all-prepared.	They said they were all ready.
Síðan hlupu þeir upp eina nátt frá skipum, þrír tigir manna saman, allir vopnaðir, og komu að bænum og var þar autt allt.	Then ran they up one night from the-ship, three tens of-men together, all weaponed, and came to dwelling and were there empty all.	They hurried up one night from the ship, and thirty men together, all armed, came to the dwelling but it was all empty.
Þórarinn hét bóndi sá er þar bjó.	Thorarin was-named a-farmer that was there settled.	Thorarin was the name of the farmer that was settled there.
Ketill mælti:	Ketil said:	Ketil said:
"Eigi hefir mitt ráð vel gefist"	"Not has my advice well given"	"My advice has not given well"
og fara síðan í burt frá bænum og ofan á leið til skipa og var þar hrísótt er þeir fóru.	and went then to away from the-dwelling and over to the-way to the-ships and were there shrubs where they went.	and then went away from the dwelling and over to the ships, and there were shrubs along where they went.
Þá mælti Ketill:	Then said Ketil:	Then Ketil said:
"Syfjar mig",	"Sleepy me",	"I feel sleepy",
sagði hann, "og verð eg að sofa".	said he, "and deserve I to sleep".	he said, "and I deserve to sleep".
Þeir kváðu það ekki mjög ráðlegt	They said that not much advisable	They said that it was not advisable,
en þó lagðist hann niður og sofnaði en þeir sátu yfir.	but though laid he down and slept while they sat over.	but he laid down and slept while they sat and watched over.
Litlu síðar vaknaði hann og mælti:	Little later awoke he and said:	A little later he awoke and said:
"Mart hefir fyrir mig borið.	"Many have before me brought.	"Much has brought before me.

The Tale of the Greenlanders (II) (The Tale of Einarr Sokkason) (Old Icelandic)

Old Icelandic	Literal	English
Hvað mun varða þótt vér kippum upp hríslu þessi er hér er undir höfði mér?"	What should happen though we jerk up clump this that here is under head mine?"	What would happen if we jerked up this clump that is here under my head?"
Þeir kipptu upp hríslunni og var þar undir jarðhús mikið.	They pulled up the-branch and was there under earth-house great.	They pulled up the branches and under it was a great cave.
Ketill mælti:	Ketil said:	Ketil said:
"Vitum fyrst hvað hér er fanga".	"Know-we first what here is provisions".	"We should know first what provisions are here".
Þeir fundu þar sex tigi sláturgripa og tólf vættir smjörs, skreið mikla.	They found there six tens carcasses and twelve weights of-butter, fish much.	They found sixty carcasses, twelve weights of butter, and a lot of fish.
"Vel er það",	"Well is that",	"That is good",
sagði Ketill, "að eg hefi eigi villt upp borið fyrir yður".	said Ketil, "that I have not wildly up presented for you".	said Ketil, "that I have not wildly brought up for you".
Nú fara þeir til skips með feng sinn.	Now went they to the-ships with provisions theirs.	Now they went to the ships with their provisions.
Nú líður að sáttarfundinum og komu hvorirtveggju til þess fundar, kaupmenn og landsmenn.	Now passed to reconciliation-meeting and came either-side to this meeting, trading-men and lands-men.	Now it passed to the reconciliation meeting, and both sides came to the meeting, the merchants and the landsmen.
Þá mælti Hallur:	Then said Hall:	Then Hall said:
"Sú er sáttargerð mín yðvar í milli að eg vil að á standist víg Össurar og Einars en fyrir manna minna mun koma sektir Austmanna, að þeir skulu hér ekki eiga vist né væri.	"So is settlement mine yours in between that I will to a to-stand slaying Ossur and Einar but for men less would come penalty Eastern-men, that they shall here not own resources nor should-they.	"This is my settlement among you, that I wish for the killing of Ossur to stand for that of Einar, but for the loss of men, the Norwegians shall not be here nor shall they own resources here.
Þau víg skulu og jöfn vera, Steingríms bónda og Símonar, Kráks austmanns og Þorfinns Grænlendings, Víghvats austmanns og Bjarnar Grænlendings, Þóris og Þórðar.	Those killings shall and even be, Steingrim's farmer and Simon, Krak the-Easterner and Thorfin The-Greenlander, Vighvats the-Easterner and Bjarn The-Greenlander, Thori and Thord.	Those killings shall be even, Steingrim the farmer and Simon, Krak the Easterner and Thorfin the Greenlander, Vighvats the Easterner and Bjarn the Greenlander, Thori and Thord.

The Tale of the Grœnlanders (II) (The Tale of Einarr Sokkason) (Old Icelandic)

Old Icelandic	Literal	English
Nú er einn óbættur vor maður er Þóarinn heitir, ómegðarmaður.	Now that one uncompensated our man that Thorarin is-named, poor-man.	Now one of our men is uncompensated, named Thorarin, a poor man.
Hann skal fé bæta".	He shall wealth be-compensated".	He shall be compensated with wealth".
Sokki hvað sér þungt gerðir líka og svo öðrum Grænlendingum er þannig fór um mannjafnað.	Sokki that himself unhappy made alike and so other Greenlanders that that-way went about equal-man.	Sokki said that he was unhappy with how it was done that Greenlanders and the other men were equally paired in that way.
Hallur kvaðst ætla að þar muni þó staðar nema hans ummæli	Hall said intend that there should though stand taking his about-matter	Hall said he intended that it should though stand as he took the matter,
og við það skildu þeir.	and with that separated they.	and with that they separated.
Síðan rak ís að og þakti alla fjörðu og hugðu Grænlendingar þá gott til ef þeir mættu taka þá og þeir færu eigi svo burt sem mælt var.	Then drifted ice to and covered all the-fjord and thought The-Greenlanders then good to of they might take then and they travel alone so away as told were.	Then ice drifted in and covered the whole fjord, and the Greenlanders thought it would be good if they could take them and they didn't go away as they were told.
En við það sjálft að mánaðarmótið kom þá rak í burt allan ísinn og gaf kaupmönnum burt af Grænlandi og skildu við það.	But with that itself to month's-end came then drove to way all ice and gave the-trading-men away of Greenland and separated with it.	But as soon as the end of the month came, all the ice was swept away and the merchants left Greenland and parted with it.
Þeir komu við Noreg.	They came to Norway.	They came to Norway.
Kolbeinn hafði haft einn hvítabjörn af Grænlandi og fór með dýrið á fund Haralds konungs gilla og gaf honum og tjáði fyrir konungi hversu þungs hlutar Grænlendingar voru af verðir og færði þá mjög í róg.	Kolbein had had one white-bear of Greenland and went with the-animal to meet Harald the-king residence and gave him and told for the-kind how-so heavily lot The-Greenlanders were of being and brought them much to slander.	Kolbein had had one white bear from Greenland and took the animal to King Harald's meeting and gave it to him and expressed to the king how much of a burden the Greenlanders were becoming and brought them into great slander.
En konungur spurði annað síðar og þótti honum Kolbeinn hafa fals fyrir sig borðið og komu engi laun fyrir dýrið.	But the-king learned otherwise later and thought he Kolbein had a-falsehood for him bore-up and came no reward for the-animal.	But the king learned otherwise later and it seemed to him that Kolbein had borne up a falsehood for him and there was no reward for the animal.

The Tale of the Greenlanders (II) (The Tale of Einarr Sokkason) (Old Icelandic)

Old Icelandic	Literal	English
Síðan hljóp Kolbeinn í flokk með Sigurði slembidjákn og gekk inn að Haraldi konungi gilla og veitti honum áverka.	Then ran Kolbein to grouped with Sigurd the-false-deacon and went in to Harald the-king residence and granted to-him a-wound.	Then Kolbein hurried to group with Sigurd the false deacon, and went into King Harald's residence and gave him a wound.
Og síðan er þeir fóru fyrir Danmörk og sigldu mjög en Kolbeinn var á eftirbáti en veður hvasst þá sleit frá bátinn og drukknaði Kolbeinn.	And then when they travelled to Denmark and sailed much but Kolbein was in the-boat-behind but weather stormy then tore-up from the-boat and drowned Kolbein.	And then when they travelled to Denmark their sail was carried much, but Kolbein was in the boat behind in stormy weather which then tore up the boat behind and Kolbein drowned.
En þeir Hermundur komu til Íslands til ættjarða sinna.	But they The-Hermunds came to Iceland to homelands theirs.	But Hermund and the others came to Iceland, their homeland.
Og lýkur þar þessi sögu.	And ends here this saga.	And here ends this saga.

Word List *(Old Icelandic to English)*

Old Icelandic	English

A, a

að	a, at, by, in, it, of, that, the, to
aðrir	other
af	from, from, of, of, off
aflað	gain
aftur	back
agir	desirable
albúnir	all-prepared
alla	all
allan	all
allir	all, all
allmjög	all-great
allt	all
allvel	all-well, all-well
andaðist	died, died
andviðri	the-storm
annað	another, another, anything-else, other, other, otherwise
annaðhvort	other-either
annarra	other
Arnald	Arnald (name)
Arnaldur	Arnald (name)
Arnbjarnar	Arnbjarn (name), Arnbjarn (name), Arnbjarnar (name)
Arnbjörn	Arnbjorn (name), Arnbjorn (name)
atburði	events
atgervi	plan
auðið	possible
austmaður	Eastern-man
austmanna	Eastern-men
austmanns	the-Easterner, the-Easterner
austmenn	Eastern-men
autt	empty

Á, á

á	a, about, and, as, at, in, of, on, out, that, the, to
áðu	that
áður	after, before
árós	river-mouth
átt	had, had, owned
áttu	had, have
áverka	a-wound

Æ, æ

æðimaður	of-mind
æpa	shouting
ætla	intend, intended, suppose, supposed
ætlaðir	intended
ætlan	intention
ætluðu	supposed
ætti	had
ættjarða	homelands

B, b

bað	asked, bid
báðir	both
báðu	asked
bæ	a-farm
bæði	asked
bægði	prevented
bæn	bidding, prayers
bænar	prayers
bændur	farmers
bænum	dwelling, the-dwelling
bæta	be-compensated
bak	back
bana	death, killed
banahögg	death-blow
banasár	death-wounds
bar	bore
bardaga	battle
barkann	throat

Word List (Old Icelandic to English)

Old Icelandic	English
báru	carried
bátinn	the-boat
bauð	asked-for, invited
beiddi	bid
bein	bones
beinum	bones
bera	bear
berast	bear
berdreyman	clear-dreams
berjast	fight
best	best
betur	better
biskuð	the-bishop
biskup	a-bishop, bishop, the-bishop
biskupi	the-bishop
biskups	bishop, the-bishop, the-bishop's
biskupsefni	the-bishop-elect
biskupslaust	bishop-less
biskupsstólinum	the-bishop's-seat
biskupsstóll	bishop's-seat
biskupsstólnum	the-bishop's-seat
biskupsstólsins	bishop's-seat
biskupsvígslu	bishop's-appointment
bjarga	rescuing
bjargar	rescue
Bjarnar	Bjarn (name)
bjarndýri	a-bear
bjó	lived, prepared, settled
bjóðast	offer
björg	rocks
bjóst	prepared
boðið	offering
bokki	buck
bol	the-trunk
bónda	farmer
bóndi	a-farmer, farmer
borð	boards, the-tables
borðið	bore-up, the-table
borðum	the-tables
borið	borne, brought, presented
borin	brought
borinn	carried
bótalausir	boat-lose
Brandur	Brand (name)
brang	chest
Brattahlíð	Brattahlid (place)
bréfum	briefs
brekku	the-slope
brekkunni	the-slope
brenndu	burned
bróðir	brother
brotið	broken
brott	away
brugðið	upset
brynjunni	the-armour
búa	prepared
búð	booth
búið	prepared, settled
búinn	prepared
búnað	preparations
búnaði	equipment, preparations
búnaður	equipment
búnir	prepared
burt	away, way
burtu	away
byggðina	the-settlement
býr	prepared
byrinn	bearing

D, d

dæma	deemed
dæmdi	judged
dag	the-day
Danmerkur	Denmark (place)
Danmörk	Denmark (place)
dauða	dead
dauður	dead
daun	the-dead
dignuðu	pride
dómi	court, the-court
dóminum	the-court
dómur	judgement
dómurinn	the-judgement
dráp	killing
draum	dream

Word List (Old Icelandic to English)

Old Icelandic	English
drauminn	the-dream
drepa	killing
dreymdi	dreamed
drukknaði	drowned
duga	aided
dyljast	hiding
dýrið	the-animal

E, e

Old Icelandic	English
eða	but, or
eðli	nature
ef	if, of
efldur	strengthened
eftir	after, afterwards, followed, following, later, remaining
eftirbáti	the-boat-behind
eftirbátinn	the-after-boat
eg	I
eið	oath
eiðar	oath
Eiði	Eid (place)
eiðrofa	breach-of-oath
eiga	have, not, own
eigi	alone, no, not
eign	property
eigna	property
eignum	owning
ein	one
eina	one
einangur	alone-going
Einar	Einar (name)
Einari	Einar (name)
Einars	Einar (name), Einar's, Einar's (name)
Einarsfjörð	Einarsfjord (place)
einhverju	one-occasion
einn	a, alone, one
einni	alone
einræði	self-will
einu	one
einum	one
Eiríksfjörð	Eriksfjord (place)
ekki	none, not
eldstóar	fire-place
en	and, as, but, than, while
enda	and
endemi	unheard-of
engi	no, no-one
engum	no
enn	but, one, still
er	are, as, be, but, is, it, that, the, then, was, we-are, what, when, where, who, with
erfitt	difficult
erindi	errand
erindis	errand
erkibiskup	the-archbishop
erkibiskups	archbishop
eru	are, are-they, they-are, were
eruð	are
Eyjafjöllum	Eyjafjolls (place)

F, f

Old Icelandic	English
fá	get
færa	bring
færði	brought
færi	going, go-to
færu	travel
færum	travel
fagra	the-fairest
fálega	coolly
falla	fall
fallinn	fallen, weak
fals	a-falsehood
fang	resources
fanga	provisions
fangið	to-catch
fangs	captivity
fara	going, travel, went, went
fari	go
farið	going
fastmæli	opinion
fé	wealth
feðgar	father-and-son

Word List (Old Icelandic to English)

Old Icelandic	English
fégjöfum	fee-gifts
féið	wealth
fékk	got, went
félaga	companions
félagar	companions
féll	fell
feng	provisions
fengju	would-get
fengu	got
fer	went
ferð	journey
ferjuna	the-ferry
ferleg	fair
festa	fix
févon	fee-trust
fimmtán	fifteen
fjár	money
fjárfundinn	wealth-finding
fjarri	far
fjölmenni	following-men, many-people
fjörðinn	fjord
fjörðu	the-fjord
fleiri	more
flokk	grouped
fólk	folk
föngum	resources
fór	for, travelled, went
forbrekkis	downhill
forn	of-old
forsjá	foresight
fóru	travelled, went
fórum	travel, travelled
förum	go
fóstbróðir	foster-brother
fótum	feet
frá	away-from, from
frænda	kinsman
frændi	kinsman
frændur	kinsmen
fram	from
framkvæmd	execution
frammi	from
fremi	provided
fréttu	found-out
fritt	peace
fróði	learned
fulltingis	assistance
fulltingja	fulfil
fulltings	help
fund	meet, meeting
fundar	meet, meeting
fundið	found
fundu	found
fúsari	willing
fylgdi	follow, followed
fylgdinni	following
fylgir	followed
fyrir	before, for, foremost, through, to
fyrirgert	before-done
fyrirkveðast	refusing
fyrr	for
fyrst	first, firstly
fýsa	desire

G, g

Old Icelandic	English
gaf	gave
gafst	gave
gamall	old
ganga	go, going, went
garða	Gardar (place)
gefa	give
gefast	give
gefist	given
gefnar	given
gegna	pass
gegnt	opposite
gegnum	through
gekk	went
gengið	been, going, walked
gengu	went
gengur	went
gera	be, be-done, do, doing, done, make, to-do, to-give
gerði	did
gerðir	made
gerðist	became
gerðu	did, done, to-do

Word List (Old Icelandic to English)

Old Icelandic	English
geri	make
gerir	make
gersemi	treasure
gerst	done
gert	done, made
get	get
getu	ability
gildur	valid
gilla	residence
gjalds	payment
góð	good
góða	good
góðan	good
góðgirnd	good-will
góður	good
göngu	going
Görðum	Gardar (place)
gott	good
grænland	Greenland (place)
Grænlendinga	Greenland (place), Greenlanders (name), the-Greenlanders'
grænlendingar	Greenlanders (name), the-Greenlanders
grænlendings	the-Greenlander
Grænlendingum	Greenland (place), Greenlanders (name)
grænlensk	Greenlandic (name)
grænlenskum	Greenlandic (name)
grænlenskur	a-Greenlander
grafa	grave
grafin	in-the-grave
greiða	assistance
greiðast	paying
greiðslu	compensation
gripagjaldið	the-artefact-fee
gripi	treasure
gripina	treasure
guði	priest
guðs	god's

H, h

Old Icelandic	English
hægra	right
haf	sea
hafa	had, has, have
hafði	had
hafi	had
hafið	have
hafskip	sea-going-ship
haft	had, has
hag	circumstances
hagkeypi	good-bargain
hagur	handy
halda	hold, rather, to-hold
haldi	hold
haldið	holding
halls	Hall's, Hall's (name)
Hallur	Hall (name)
hamarrifu	crags
hámessu	high-mass
hann	he, him
hans	him, his, its
haraldi	Harald (name)
haralds	Harald (name)
harmaði	harmed
hásetar	the-crew
haustum	autumn
hefði	had
hefðu	had
hefi	have
hefir	has, has-been, have
hegna	protected
heim	home
heimamaður	house-man
heimilisprestur	local-priest
heimta	carry
heimti	presented
heita	be-called
heitir	is-named
heitukötlum	boiling-cauldrons
héldu	held
heldur	rather
hendi	hand
hendur	hand
henta	suitable
hér	here
herða	shoulders
Hermundur	Hermund (name), the-Hermunds (name)
herra	sir

Word List (Old Icelandic to English)

Old Icelandic	English	Old Icelandic	English
hést	promised	horfir	looks, where
hét	named, was-named	hríð	time
heyra	hear	hrinda	repel
heyrðu	heard	hringdi	called
heyrt	heard	hringja	call
hið	the, then	hríslu	clump
hingað	here	hríslunni	the-branch
hinir	others	hrísótt	shrubs
hinn	the	hugðu	thought
hinu	the	hugi	his-mind
hitta	find	hugur	mind
hitti	found, met	hún	she
hittust	found, met	hurðina	the-door
hjá	beside, by	húsa	house
hjó	struck	hvað	that, what
hlaðna	loaded	hvar	where
hlaupa	running	hvasst	stormy
hleypið	discharge	hver	each, who
hleypir	released	hverfa	turn
hleypur	ran	hverju	how
hlífast	protect	hversu	how-so
hlítt	satisfactory	hvítabjörn	white-bear
hljóp	ran	Hvítserk	Hvitserk (name)
hlupu	ran	hvorirtveggju	either-side
hlut	lot, part	hvors	which
hlutar	lot	hvort	each, whether
hlutum	things	hvortveggji	each
hnjóðhamar	hammer	hvoru	each
höfðaskip	a-headed-ship	hvorum	each
höfðaskipið	head-ship	hygg	think
höfði	head		
höfðingja	chieftains		
höfðu	had, had-they, they-had	**I, i**	
höfuð	head	illa	angry, ill
höfuðgjarnt	headstrong	illt	ill
höfuðsmenn	head-men	inn	in
höfum	have	inni	in
hoggið	struck	innsiglum	seals
höggva	to-strike		
holdi	flesh	**Í, í**	
Holtavatnsós	Holtavatnsos (place)		
hönd	hand		
höndum	handling	í	about, and, at, in, into, of, on, that, to
honum	he, him, his, to-him	ís	ice
horfðu	looked		

Word List (Old Icelandic to English)

Old Icelandic	English
Ísa-Steingrímur	Isa-Steingrim (name)
ísinn	ice
Íslandi	Iceland (place)
Íslands	Iceland (place)

J, j

Old Icelandic	English
jafnsnemma	equally-early
jafnt	equal
jarða	earthed
jarðhús	earth-house
játtuðu	agreed
jöfn	even
jöklinum	a-glacier
jöklum	glaciers
Jórsalafari	Jerusalem-Traveller (name)

K, k

Old Icelandic	English
kæmi	comes
Kálfsson	son-of-Kalf (name)
kalla	call, claim
kallaði	called
kallar	called
kambi	comb
kann	can
kastaði	cast
kaupmenn	the-merchants, the-trading-men, trading-men
kaupmennirnir	the-trading-men
kaupmönnum	the-trading-men, trading-men
kaupskip	merchant-ship
kaupskipið	merchant-ship
kaupskipin	merchant-ships
kaupum	a-deal
kemst	come
kennimanns	teaching
kennimenn	priests
kerling	old-woman
kerlingu	the-old-woman
Ketil	Ketil (name)
Ketill	Ketil (name)
Ketils	Ketil (name), Ketil's (name)
Kiðjabergs	Kidjaberg (place)
kilinum	the-keel
kipptu	pulled
kippum	jerk
kirkju	church, the-church
kirkjugarðsins	churchyard
kirkjumessu	church-mass
kirkjuna	the-church
kirkjuvegginn	church-wall
klerkur	cleric
knjám	knees
Koðránsson	son-of-Kodran (name)
Kolbein	Kolbein (name)
Kolbeini	Kolbein (name)
Kolbeinn	Kolbein (name)
Kolbeins	Kolbein (name)
kom	came
koma	come
komast	came, come
komið	come
kominn	come, coming
komst	came
komu	came
komust	came
konung	the-king
konungi	the-kind, the-king
konungs	the-king, the-king's
konungsbréfum	the-king's-brief
konungur	the-king
kostur	choice
Kráks	Krak (name)
kunni	known
kunnig	known
kvað	said
kvaðst	said
kváðu	said, saying
kváðust	said
kveðið	declared
kveðja	called
kveðst	said
kveld	night
kyrrrlátir	still
kyrrt	still

Word List (Old Icelandic to English)

Old Icelandic	English

L, l

Old Icelandic	English
lá	lay
lagðist	laid
lagður	laid
land	land
Landeyjum	the-Landeys (place)
landi	the-land
landið	the-land
landsins	the-lands
landsmenn	lands-men
landsmönnum	lands-men
Langanes	Langanes (place)
láta	lay-out
laun	reward
legðu	put
leggja	allow, have, lay
leggur	propose
legið	laid
leið	the-way
leit	looked
leita	seek
lengi	long
lengra	longer
lengur	longer
lést	had
lét	had, laid, laid-out
létu	had
leyndust	innermost
leynivogi	hidden-creek
leysti	released
lið	team
liði	company, team
liðið	passed
liðskost	force
liðu	passed
líður	passed
liðveislu	support
líftjóni	loss-of-life
lík	the-body
líka	alike, like
líkaði	liked
líkar	like, likes
líkast	likely
líkhringingu	funeral-procession
líkhringinguna	the-funeral-procession
líkindi	alike
líkinu	the-body
líklegast	likely
líkum	bodies
líst	behold
lítið	little
lítil	little
lítillæti	humility
litlu	little
lítt	little
lög	law, laws
lögðu	laid
lögum	law
Lund	Lund (place)
lýkur	ends

M, m

Old Icelandic	English
maður	a-man, man
mæla	badly
mælt	told
mælti	said, spoke
mæltu	said
mætti	might
mættir	might
mættu	might
maklegast	most
mal	the-matter
mál	a-case, case, matter, matters, the-case, the-matter
málahlutur	matter-lot
máli	discuss, the-matter
málið	the-case
málsfyllingar	the-matter-fulfilling
málum	case, cases, matter, the-matter
málunum	the-matter
mánaðarmótið	month's-end
mann	a-man, man, the-man
manna	man's, men, of-men, peoples'

Word List (Old Icelandic to English)

Old Icelandic	English
manndómsleysi	meanness
mannhættu	dangerous
manni	man
manninum	this-man
mannjafnað	equal-man
mannshræ	dead-body, human-body
mannvænlegur	a-friendly
margt	many
mart	many
mat	food
mátti	might
með	with
meðallagi	moderately
meðan	as-long-as, while
mega	may
megin	sides
megri	meagre
mein	disease, harm
meir	more
meira	more
meiri	more
menn	lessened, men, people
mér	I, me, mine, to-me
messu	mass
mest	most
mestur	the-most
metnir	important
metorð	esteem
miðju	the-middle
mig	me
mikið	a-great, great, many, much
mikil	great, much
mikill	great, much
mikils	much
mikinn	much
mikla	great, large, much
miklir	much
miklu	much
milli	between
mín	mine
minn	mine
minna	less
minni	less, mine
minnka	decreased
mínum	mine, my
misst	lost
mitt	my
mjög	much, very
mönnum	men, the-men
morguninn	morning
mót	meet, meeting
móti	facing
mun	may, should, will, will-be, would
muna	remember
mundi	would
mundu	should, would, would-be
mundum	would
muni	should, will, would
munni	mouth
munt	would
muntu	shall-you
munu	shall, should, would
munum	shall

N, n

Old Icelandic	English
náðu	reached
næði	get
nær	as-far, close, nearer
næst	next
nætur	night, the-night
náir	getting
nátt	night
nauðsyn	necessary, needs
né	nor
neðan	below
nema	taking
nenna	bothered
nes	headland
niður	down
Njálsson	son-of-Njal (name)
nokkuð	some
nokkur	some
nokkura	some
nokkurar	some
nokkurn	some

Word List (Old Icelandic to English)

Old Icelandic	English
nokkurra	something
nokkuru	some
nokkurum	some
Noreg	Norway (place)
noregi	Norway (place)
Noregs	Norway (place)
norrænir	Nordic (name)
norrænn	Nordic (name)
nótt	the-night
nú	not, now
nytjum	use

O, o

Old Icelandic	English
Odda	Odda (place)
of	of
ofan	above, over
ofsa	violence
ofsamenn	overbearing-men
oft	often
og	also, and
orð	a-word, word, words
orða	words
orðið	become, have-become
orðinn	the-words
orðsending	word-sending
oss	to-us, us

Ó, ó

Old Icelandic	English
óbættur	uncompensated
óbyggðir	un-settled
óbyggðum	the-unsettled-land
óðir	angry
óforsjáll	impulsive
ófús	reluctant
ójafnað	un-equal
ójafnaður	unequal
ómegðarmaður	poor-man
ósæmd	dishonourable
ósett	unsettled
óþekktarsvip	dishonourable, ungraceful

Old Icelandic	English
óvirðing	un-worthy
óvíst	uncertain

Ö, ö

Old Icelandic	English
öðru	another, other
öðrum	other, others
öllu	all
öllum	all, ill
ört	swiftly
Össur	Ossur (name)
Össurar	of-Ossur (name), Ossur (name)
Össuri	Ossur (name)
öx	an-axe, axe
öxarhyrnunni	axe-horn
öxi	an-axe, axe

R, r

Old Icelandic	English
ráð	advice, advisable, decide
ráða	advice
ráðast	arrange, be-arranged
ráðist	advise
ráðlegt	advisable
ráðum	advice
rak	drifted, drove
raunar	actually
réð	commanded
réðist	deal
réðst	ruled
refsa	punish
reið	rode
reiðisvipur	angry
reiður	angry
reikaði	wandered
rétt	rights
réttara	more-correct
réttlegast	correctness
reyndust	gave-him
rísi	giants
rjúfa	break-open
róg	slander

Word List (Old Icelandic to English)

Old Icelandic	English
róstu	uproar
rufu	broke-up, tore-up

S, s

Old Icelandic	English
sá	saw, so, that
sægarpur	sea-champion
sækja	seek, sought
sæmd	honour
sæmdar	honour
sæmdir	honour
Sæmundi	Saemund (name)
Sæmundur	Saemund (name)
sætt	settled
sættast	reconcile
sættir	reconciliation
sættirnar	reconciliation
sætu	reconcile
sagði	said, said
sagt	said, said, told
sakir	sake
sáluhjápar	souls
sálum	souls
sama	same
saman	altogether, together
sami	same
samt	the-same, together
sanni	the-truth
sannlegast	truthfully
sannyrði	true-words
sárir	wounded
sat	sat
satt	TRUE
sáttarfund	peace-meeting
sáttarfundinum	reconciliation-meeting
sáttargerð	settlement
sátu	sat, sat
sáu	saw, saw
sauminn	the-seam
sé	being, him, is, this, to-be
segið	say
segir	said, say, says
segja	say
seinka	delay
sektir	penalty
sem	as
senda	send
sendi	sent
sendilegastan	to-be-sent
sér	as, him, himself, them, themselves
sett	sat, set, settled
setti	set
settur	set
settust	sat
séu	are, they-are
sex	six
síðan	then
síðar	later
síðast	last
sig	him, himself
sígast	sinking
sigldu	sailed
sigur	victory
Sigurði	Sigurd (name)
Sigurður	Sigurd (name)
Símon	Simon (name)
Símonar	Simon (name)
símoni	Simon (name), Simon's (name)
sín	him, his, theirs
sína	his, their, themselves
sinn	his, theirs
sinna	his, theirs
sinni	his, they
síns	his
sínu	his, theirs
sínum	his, theirs
sitja	sit
sitt	his, this
sjá	saw, see
sjálfs	himself
sjálft	itself
sjást	looked
skal	shall
skála	cabin
skáladyrnar	the-door
skálann	the-cabin, the-hut
skálanum	the-cabin
skammt	a-short-distance

Word List (Old Icelandic to English)

Old Icelandic	English
skaplyndi	temper
skapraun	temperament
skerast	cutting
skildu	parted, separated
skilja	part
skip	ship
skipa	the-ships
skipi	ship, the-ship
skipið	ship, the-ship
skipinu	the-ship
skips	ships, the-ships
skiptu	divided
skipum	ships, the-ship
skipverjar	crew
Skjálgsbúða	Skjalgsbud (place)
skjótlega	shortly
skjótt	away
skreið	fish
skuli	shall
skulu	shall
skyldi	should, should-be
skyldir	should
skyldu	should, would
slær	struck
slæst	slipped
sláturgripa	carcasses
sleit	tore-up
slembidjákn	the-false-deacon
slík	such
slíka	such
slíkan	such
slíks	such
slíkt	such
slíku	such
slíkum	such
slógu	strike
smáskipum	small-ships
smjörs	of-butter
snaraðist	caught-up
snerist	turned
snúast	return
sofa	sleep
sofnaði	slept
sögðu	said
sögu	saga
Sokka	Sokki (name)
Sokkason	son-of-Sokki (name)
Sokki	Sokki (name)
Sólarfjöllum	Solarfjoll (place)
son	son
söng	sang
sóttu	sought
spangabrynja	plate-mail
spillt	damaged
spretta	sprang
spurði	learned
spurðist	heard-of
spurðu	heard-of
spurðust	heard-of
spurt	learned
spyrjast	known-about
stað	stand
staðar	stand
staðarins	of-the-place, the-place
staðið	stood
stakk	thrust
standa	stand
standist	to-stand
stefnur	plans
steig	stepped
steinda	stone-one
Steingríms	Steingrim's (name)
Steingrímur	Steingrim (name)
steint	stone-carving
Steinþór	Steinthor (name)
stendur	standing
sterkur	strong
stóð	standing, stood
stofuna	sitting-room
stokk	a-log
stökki	blood-splattered
stól	seat
stórfjörðu	large-fjords
stórir	badly
stórskipum	large-ships
stórvirki	great-works
studdist	stood
stukku	went-away
stutt	supported
stýrimaður	steersman

Word List (Old Icelandic to English)

Old Icelandic	English	*Old Icelandic*	English
stýrimanns	steersman	tíðinda	news
styrktarmaður	supporter	tíðindi	news, tidings
sú	so	tíðindin	the-news
suður	south	tíðindum	news
sumarið	summer	tigi	tens
sumars	summer	tigir	tens
sumir	some	tignar	position
sumri	of-summer	til	the, to, until
sumur	summers	tilstilli	agency, guidance
sunnan	to-the-south	tindinn	pin
svara	answered	tjáði	spoke, told, voiced
svarar	answered	tjald	tent
svardaga	oath	tjalda	tent-up
sveit	company, the-company	tók	took
		tóku	took
sveitunga	men-company	tólf	twelve
sverði	to-the-sword	tóm	time
sverji	swear	tómlega	time-like
sviptur	deprived	torsóttlegt	difficult
svívirðing	disgrace	traust	trust
svívirðlega	disgracefully	troða	tread
svo	so	tveim	two
svörð	skins	tvö	two
syfjar	sleepy	týnst	lost
sýndi	showed		
sýndist	seemed		
syngja	sing, sung		
sýnir	showed		
sýnist	seems		
sýnt	shown		
systurson	sister's-son		

Þ, þ

		þá	them, then, when
		það	it, that, the, this, to
		þakkaði	thanked
		þakti	covered
		þangað	from-then, from-there
		þann	that, then
		þannig	that-way
		þar	here, that, then, there
		þau	then, those
		þegar	instantly, straightaway, straight-away, them
		þeim	of-them, theirs, them, they, to-them
		þeir	they, was
		þeirra	of-them, theirs, them, they
		þeirrar	their

T, t

taka	take, took
taki	take
tala	spoke
talaði	told
tannvöru	walrus-tusks
tekið	taken
tekinn	taken
tekna	taken
teknir	taken
tíða	the-service
tíðamanni	worshippers

Word List (Old Icelandic to English)

Old Icelandic	English
þennan	then
þér	to-you, you
þess	this
þessa	this
þessi	these, this
þessir	these
þessu	this
þessum	these, this
þetta	it, that, this
þig	you
þiggja	accepted
þín	your
þína	yours
þing	assembly
þings	assembly, the-assembly
þjónustumenn	servants-of
þó	though
Þóarinn	Thorarin (name)
Þórarinn	Thorarin (name)
Þórðar	Thord (name)
Þórðarson	son-of-Thord (name)
Þórði	Thord's (name)
Þórður	Thord (name)
Þorfinns	Thorfin (name)
Þorgils	Thorgils (name)
Þóris	Thori (name)
Þórisson	son-of-Thorri (name)
Þorljótsson	son-of-Thorljot (name)
þótt	though
þótti	thought
þóttist	thought
þriðja	third, thirdly
þrír	three
þrjá	three
þú	you
þunglegar	the-more-difficult
þungs	heavily
þungt	unhappy
þverra	running-out
því	according, accordingly, as, because, because-of, that, then, therefore, they
þvo	washed
þykir	seems
þykist	seems
þyrfti	needed

U, u

Old Icelandic	English
ullkamb	wool-comb
um	about, around
umdæmi	about-judgement
umdæmis	area
ummæli	about-matter
umræða	discussed
una	content
undan	away-from
undarlegt	strange
undir	submit, under
uni	like
unna	win
unum	among
upp	up
uppgefnir	up-given
uppi	up
urðu	became

Ú, ú

Old Icelandic	English
úfar	misfortune
úr	from, out-from, out-of
úrræði	solution
úrræðið	solution
út	out
úti	outside
útlenda	foreign

V, v

Old Icelandic	English
vægja	make-peace
vænleg	hopeful
vænta	hoped
vænti	expect
væntu	expected

Word List (Old Icelandic to English)

Old Icelandic	English
væri	be, should-be, should-they, to-be, was
vættir	weights
vaknaði	awoke
vald	power
vanda	problem
vandi	custom
vanfær	unable
vanist	custom
vanmeginn	weak
var	was, were
varð	became, came
varða	happen
varist	weariness
varla	hardly
varnarmaður	defender
varning	wares
varúðgir	cautious
vaskir	brave
veður	weather
vegna	slain
veiðiskap	hunting
veislu	feast
veislunni	the-feast
veit	know, knowing
veita	grant
veitti	granted
vel	well
veld	willed
veldur	brought-about, caused
vér	us, we, we-are
vera	be, being, to-be, would-be
verð	deserve
verða	be, become
verði	be
verðið	become
verðir	being
verður	becomes
verið	been
verk	work
verum	we
vestan	western
Vestribyggð	Vestribyggd (place)
Vestribyggðar	Vestribyggd (place)
veturinn	winter
við	by, to, with
víða	widely
viðbúnað	preparation
viðinn	the-trees
víg	killings, slaying
vígði	consecrated
Víghvats	Vighvats (name)
vígi	battle
vígið	killing
vígsgengi	in-battle
vil	will, wish
vildi	wanted, willed
vildu	willed
vilja	willed, wished-for
viljum	wish
villt	wildly
vini	friends
vinsæll	popular
virðing	worthiness
virðingar	worthiness
virðum	worthiness
virður	respected
vís	aware
vissu	know
vist	resources
víst	certainly
vistföng	resources
vistir	supplies
vistunum	provisions
vitrum	wise
vitum	know-we
vitur	wise
viturlega	wise-like
völlinn	the-field
von	expect, expected, hope
vopnaðir	weaponed
vor	our, ours, spring, us
vorið	spring
vorkunn	pity
vorn	our, ours
vorri	ours
voru	was, were

Word List (Old Icelandic to English)

Old Icelandic   English

Y, y

yðru	your
yður	you
yðvar	you, yours
yðvarn	with-you
yfir	over
yfirbóta	over-compensation
yrði	become, would
yrðu	be

Ý, ý

ýldu	decay

Word List *(English to Old Icelandic)*

English	Old Icelandic
A, a	
a	á, á, á
about	á, á, á
and	á, á, á, á, að
as	á, á, á, að, að, að
at	á, á, að
after	áður, áður
all-prepared	albúnir
all	alla, allan, allir, allir, allmjög, allt, allvel
all-great	allmjög
all-well	allvel, allvel
another	annað, annað, annað
anything-else	annað
Arnald (name)	Arnald, Arnaldur
Arnbjarn (name)	Arnbjarnar, Arnbjarnar
Arnbjarnar (name)	Arnbjarnar
Arnbjorn (name)	Arnbjörn, Arnbjörn
a-wound	áverka
asked	bað, bað, báðir
a-farm	bæ
asked-for	bauð
a-bishop	biskup
a-bear	bjarndýri
a-farmer	bóndi
away	brott, búð, búnaði, búnaður
aided	duga
afterwards	eftir
alone	eigi, einangur, Einar
alone-going	einangur
are	er, er, er, er
archbishop	erkibiskups
are-they	eru
a-falsehood	fals
away-from	frá, frá
assistance	fulltingis, fulltingja
ability	getu
a-Greenlander	grænlenskur
autumn	haustum
a-headed-ship	höfðaskip
angry	illa, illa, illt, inn
agreed	játtuðu
a-glacier	jöklinum
a-deal	kaupum
allow	leggja
alike	líka, líka
a-man	maður, maður
a-case	mál
a-friendly	mannvænlegur
as-long-as	meðan
a-great	mikið
as-far	nær
above	ofan
also	og
a-word	orð
an-axe	öx, öx
axe	öx, öxarhyrnunni
axe-horn	öxarhyrnunni
advice	ráð, ráð, ráð
advisable	ráð, ráð
arrange	ráðast
advise	ráðist
actually	raunar
altogether	saman
a-short-distance	skammt
a-log	stokk
answered	svara, svarar
accepted	þiggja
assembly	þing, þings
according	því
accordingly	því
agency	tilstilli
around	um
about-judgement	umdæmi
area	umdæmis
about-matter	ummæli
among	unum
awoke	vaknaði
aware	vís

B, b

Word List (English to Old Icelandic)

English	Old Icelandic
by	að, að, að
before	áður, ætla
back	aftur, agir
bid	bað, báðir
both	báðir
bidding	bæn
be-compensated	bæta
bore	bar
battle	bardaga, báru
bones	bein, beinum
bear	bera, berast
best	best
better	betur
bishop	biskup, biskups
bishop-less	biskupslaust
bishop's-seat	biskupsstóll, biskupsstólsins
bishop's-appointment	biskupsvígslu
Bjarn (name)	Bjarnar
buck	bokki
boards	borð
bore-up	borðið
borne	borið
brought	borið, borin, borinn
boat-lose	bótalausir
Brand (name)	Brandur
Brattahlid (place)	Brattahlíð
briefs	bréfum
burned	brenndu
brother	bróðir
broken	brotið
booth	búð
bearing	byrinn
but	eða, ef, eftir, eftir
breach-of-oath	eiðrofa
be	er, er, er, er, erfitt, erindi, erindis
bring	færa
before-done	fyrirgert
been	gengið, gengið
be-done	gera
became	gerðist, gerðu, gerðu
be-called	heita
boiling-cauldrons	heitukötlum
beside	hjá
bodies	líkum
behold	líst
badly	mæla, mætti
between	milli
below	neðan
bothered	nenna
become	orðið, orðið, ósæmd, óþekktarsvip
be-arranged	ráðast
break-open	rjúfa
broke-up	rufu
being	sé, sé, sé
blood-splattered	stökki
because	því
because-of	því
brave	vaskir
brought-about	veldur
becomes	verður

C, c

English	Old Icelandic
carried	báru, bauð
clear-dreams	berdreyman
chest	brang
court	dómi
coolly	fálega
captivity	fangs
companions	félaga, félagar
compensation	greiðslu
circumstances	hag
crags	hamarrifu
carry	heimta
chieftains	höfðingja
called	hringdi, hringja, hríslu, hugi
call	hringja, hríslu
clump	hríslu
comes	kæmi
claim	kalla
comb	kambi
can	kann
cast	kastaði
come	kemst, Ketil, Ketill, Ketils, Ketils
church	kirkju
churchyard	kirkjugarðsins

Word List (English to Old Icelandic)

English	Old Icelandic	English	Old Icelandic
church-mass	kirkjumessu	done	gera, gera, gerði, gerðir
church-wall	kirkjuvegginn	did	gerði, gerðir
cleric	klerkur	discharge	hleypið
came	kom, koma, komast, komast, komið, kominn	declared	kveðið
		discuss	máli
coming	kominn	dangerous	mannhættu
choice	kostur	dead-body	mannshræ
company	liði, liðskost	disease	mein
case	mál, mál	decreased	minnka
cases	málum	down	niður
close	nær	dishonourable	ósæmd, óþekktarsvip
commanded	réð	decide	ráð
correctness	réttlegast	drifted	rak
cabin	skála	drove	rak
cutting	skerast	deal	réðist
crew	skipverjar	delay	seinka
carcasses	sláturgripa	divided	skiptu
caught-up	snaraðist	damaged	spillt
covered	þakti	deprived	sviptur
content	una	disgrace	svívirðing
custom	vandi, vanist	disgracefully	svívirðlega
cautious	varúðgir	discussed	umræða
caused	veldur	defender	varnarmaður
consecrated	vígði	deserve	verð
certainly	víst	decay	ýldu

D, d

E, e

English	Old Icelandic	English	Old Icelandic
desirable	agir	events	atburði
died	andaðist, andaðist	Eastern-man	austmaður
dwelling	bænum	Eastern-men	austmanna, austmenn
death	bana	empty	autt
death-blow	banahögg	equipment	búnaði, búnaður
death-wounds	banasár	Eid (place)	Eiði
deemed	dæma	Einar (name)	Einar, Einari, Einars
Denmark (place)	Danmerkur, Danmörk	Einar's	einars
dead	dauða, dauður	Einar's (name)	Einars
dream	draum	Einarsfjord (place)	Einarsfjörð
dreamed	dreymdi	Eriksfjord (place)	Eiríksfjörð
drowned	drukknaði	errand	erindi, erindis
difficult	erfitt, erindi	Eyjafjolls (place)	Eyjafjöllum
downhill	forbrekkis	execution	framkvæmd
desire	fýsa	each	hver, hverju, hversu, Hvítserk, hvorirtveggju
do	gera		
doing	gera	either-side	hvorirtveggju

Word List (English to Old Icelandic)

English	Old Icelandic	English	Old Icelandic
equally-early	jafnsnemma	firstly	fyrst
equal	jafnt	find	hitta
earthed	jarða	flesh	holdi
earth-house	jarðhús	force	liðskost
even	jöfn	funeral-procession	líkhringingu
ends	lýkur	food	mat
equal-man	mannjafnað	facing	móti
esteem	metorð	fish	skreið
expect	vænti, væntu	from-then	þangað
expected	væntu, væri	from-there	þangað
		foreign	útlenda
		feast	veislu
		friends	vini

F, f

G, g

English	Old Icelandic	English	Old Icelandic
from	af, af, aflað, aftur, agir, albúnir		
farmers	bændur	gain	aflað
fight	berjast	get	fá, færa, færði
farmer	bónda, bóndi	going	færi, færi, fálega, falla, fallinn, fals
followed	eftir, eftir, eftir		
following	eftir, eftir	go-to	færi
fire-place	eldstóar	go	fari, farið, feðgar
fall	falla	got	fékk, félaga
fallen	fallinn	grouped	flokk
father-and-son	feðgar	gave	gaf, gafst
fee-gifts	fégjöfum	Gardar (place)	garða, gefa
fell	féll	give	gefa, gefast
fair	ferleg	given	gefist, gefnar
fix	festa	good	góð, góða, góðan, góðgirnd, góður
fee-trust	févon		
fifteen	fimmtán	good-will	góðgirnd
far	fjarri	Greenland (place)	grænland, Grænlendinga, grænlendinga
following-men	fjölmenni		
fjord	fjörðinn		
folk	fólk	Greenlanders (name)	grænlendinga, grænlendingar, Grænlendingum
for	fór, forbrekkis, forsjá		
foresight	forsjá		
foster-brother	fóstbróðir	Greenlandic (name)	grænlensk, grænlenskum
feet	fótum		
found-out	fréttu	grave	grafa
fulfil	fulltingja	god's	guðs
found	fundið, fundu, fylgdi, fylgdi	good-bargain	hagkeypi
		glaciers	jöklum
follow	fylgdi	great	mikið, mikið, mikið, mikil
foremost	fyrir	getting	náir
first	fyrst	gave-him	reyndust

Word List (English to Old Icelandic)

English	Old Icelandic	English	Old Icelandic
giants	rísi	head-ship	höfðaskipið
great-works	stórvirki	head	höfði, höfðingja
guidance	tilstilli	had-they	höfðu
grant	veita	headstrong	höfuðgjarnt
granted	veitti	head-men	höfuðsmenn
		Holtavatnsos (place)	Holtavatnsós
		handling	höndum
		his-mind	hugi

H, h

English	Old Icelandic	English	Old Icelandic
		house	húsa
had	ætti, ættjarða, af, af, aflað, aftur, agir, albúnir, alla, allan, allir, allir, allmjög, allt	how	hverju
		how-so	hversu
		Hvítserk (name)	Hvítserk
		hidden-creek	leynivogi
homelands	ættjarða	humility	lítillæti
have	áttu, austmaður, austmanna, austmenn, autt, áverka, bað, bað	human-body	mannshræ
		harm	mein
		headland	nes
hiding	dyljast	have-become	orðið
help	fulltings	honour	sæmd, sæmdar, sæmdir
has	hafa, hafa, hafði		
handy	hagur	himself	sér, séu, síðar
hold	halda, haldi	heard-of	spurðist, spurðu, spurðust
holding	haldið		
Hall's	halls	heavily	þungs
Hall's (name)	Halls	hopeful	vænleg
Hall (name)	Hallur	hoped	vænta
high-mass	hámessu	happen	varða
he	hann, hann	hardly	varla
him	hann, hans, hans, hans, haraldi, haralds, harmaði	hunting	veiðiskap
		hope	von
his	hans, hans, haraldi, haralds, harmaði, haustum, hefði, hefðu, hefi, hefir, hefir		

I, i

English	Old Icelandic
Harald (name)	haraldi, haralds
harmed	harmaði
has-been	hefir
home	heim
house-man	heimamaður
held	héldu
hand	hendi, hendur, hér
here	hér, Hermundur, heyra
Hermund (name)	Hermundur
hear	heyra
heard	heyrðu, heyrt
hammer	hnjóðhamar

English	Old Icelandic
in	á, að, að, að, að
it	að, áður, áður, ætla
intend	ætla
intended	ætla, ætlaðir
intention	ætlan
invited	bauð
if	ef
I	eg, Eiði
is	er, er
in-the-grave	grafin
its	hans
is-named	heitir

Word List (English to Old Icelandic)

English	Old Icelandic	English	Old Icelandic
into	í	lived	bjó
ill	illa, illt, inn	later	eftir, eg
ice	ís, Ísa-Steingrímur	learned	fróði, fulltingis, fulltingja
Isa-Steingrim (name)	Ísa-Steingrímur	local-priest	heimilisprestur
Iceland (place)	íslandi, íslands	loaded	hlaðna
innermost	leyndust	lot	hlut, hlutar
important	metnir	looked	horfðu, horfir, hringdi
impulsive	óforsjáll	looks	horfir
itself	sjálft	lay	lá, lagðist
instantly	þegar	laid	lagðist, lagður, land, landsmenn, landsmönnum
in-battle	vígsgengi	land	land
		lands-men	landsmenn, landsmönnum

J, j

English	Old Icelandic
judged	dæmdi
judgement	dómur
journey	ferð
Jerusalem-Traveller (name)	Jórsalafari
jerk	kippum

English	Old Icelandic
Langanes (place)	Langanes
lay-out	láta
long	lengi
longer	lengra, lengur
laid-out	lét
loss-of-life	líftjóni
like	líka, líkaði, líkar
liked	líkaði
likes	líkar
likely	líkast, líkhringingu
little	lítið, lítil, lítillæti, litlu
law	lög, lög
laws	lög
Lund (place)	Lund
lessened	menn
large	mikla
less	minna, minni
lost	misst, mitt
last	síðast
large-fjords	stórfjörðu
large-ships	stórskipum

K, k

English	Old Icelandic
killed	bana
killing	dráp, draum, drepa
kinsman	frænda, frændi
kinsmen	frændur
Ketil (name)	Ketil, Ketill, Ketils
Ketil's (name)	Ketils
Kidjaberg (place)	Kiðjabergs
knees	knjám
Kolbein (name)	Kolbein, Kolbeini, Kolbeinn, Kolbeins
Krak (name)	Kráks
known	kunni, kunnig
known-about	spyrjast
know	veit, veit
knowing	veit
killings	víg
know-we	vitum

M, m

English	Old Icelandic
money	fjár
many-people	fjölmenni
more	fleiri, flokk, fólk, fór
meet	fund, fund, fundar
meeting	fund, fundar, fundar
make	gera, gerði, gerðir

L, l

112

Word List (English to Old Icelandic)

English	Old Icelandic
made	gerðir, gerðist
met	hitti, hittust
mind	hugur
merchant-ship	kaupskip, kaupskipið
merchant-ships	kaupskipin
man	maður, mæla, mætti
might	mætti, mættir, mættu, maklegast
most	maklegast, mál
matter	mál, mál
matters	mál
matter-lot	málahlutur
month's-end	mánaðarmótið
man's	manna
men	manna, manndómsleysi, mannhættu
meanness	manndómsleysi
many	margt, mart, mat
moderately	meðallagi
may	mega, megri
meagre	megri
me	mér, mér
mine	mér, messu, mest, metnir, metorð
mass	messu
much	mikið, mikil, mikil, mikill, mikill, mikils, mikinn, mikla, mikla
my	mínum, misst
morning	morguninn
mouth	munni
more-correct	réttara
men-company	sveitunga
misfortune	úfar
make-peace	vægja

N, n

English	Old Icelandic
nature	eðli
not	eiga, eiga, eigi, eigi
no	eigi, eigi, eign
none	ekki
no-one	engi
named	hét
night	kveld, kyrrrlátir, kyrrt
nearer	nær
next	næst
necessary	nauðsyn
needs	nauðsyn
nor	né
Norway (place)	Noreg, noregi, Noregs
Nordic (name)	norrænir, norrænn
now	nú
needed	þyrfti
news	tíðinda, tíðindi, tíðindi

O, o

English	Old Icelandic
of	á, á, á, á, á, á, að
on	á, á
out	á, á
other	aðrir, áðu, æðimaður, æpa, ætla, ætla
of-mind	æðimaður
off	af
otherwise	annað
other-either	annaðhvort
owned	átt
offer	bjóðast
offering	boðið
or	eða
oath	eið, eiðar, eiga
own	eiga
owning	eignum
one	ein, eina, einhverju, einn, einræði, einu
one-occasion	einhverju
opinion	fastmæli
of-old	forn
old	gamall
opposite	gegnt
others	hinir, hinn
old-woman	kerling
of-men	manna
Odda (place)	Odda
over	ofan, ofsa
overbearing-men	ofsamenn
often	oft
Ossur (name)	Össur, Össurar, Össurar

Word List (English to Old Icelandic)

English	Old Icelandic	English	Old Icelandic
of-Ossur (name)	Össurar	penalty	sektir
of-butter	smjörs	parted	skildu
of-the-place	staðarins	plate-mail	spangabrynja
of-summer	sumri	plans	stefnur
of-them	þeim, þeim	position	tignar
out-from	úr	pin	tindinn
out-of	úr	power	vald
outside	úti	problem	vanda
our	vor, vor	preparation	viðbúnað
ours	vor, vor, vor	popular	vinsæll
over-compensation	yfirbóta	pity	vorkunn

P, p

R, r

English	Old Icelandic	English	Old Icelandic
plan	atgervi	river-mouth	árós
possible	auðið	rescuing	bjarga
prevented	bægði	rescue	bjargar
prayers	bæn, bænar	rocks	björg
prepared	bjó, bjó, bjóðast, björg, bjóst, boðið, bol	remaining	eftir
		resources	fang, fanga, fangið, fara
presented	borið, brekku	refusing	fyrirkveðast
preparations	búnað, búnaði	residence	gilla
pride	dignuðu	right	hægra
property	eign, eigna	rather	halda, halda
provisions	fanga, fangið, fara	running	hlaupa
provided	fremi	released	hleypir, hleypur
peace	fritt	ran	hleypur, hlífast, hlítt
pass	gegna	repel	hrinda
payment	gjalds	reward	laun
paying	greiðast	remember	muna
priest	guði	reached	náðu
protected	hegna	reluctant	ófús
promised	hést	ruled	réðst
protect	hlífast	rode	reið
part	hlut, hlutum	rights	rétt
priests	kennimenn	reconcile	sættast, sættir
pulled	kipptu	reconciliation	sættir, sættirnar
put	legðu	reconciliation-meeting	sáttarfundinum
propose	leggur	return	snúast
passed	liðið, liðu, líður	running-out	þverra
peoples'	manna	respected	virður
people	menn		
poor-man	ómegðarmaður		
punish	refsa		
peace-meeting	sáttarfund		

S, s

Word List (English to Old Icelandic)

English	Old Icelandic	English	Old Icelandic
shouting	æpa	Saemund (name)	Sæmundi, Sæmundur
suppose	ætla	sake	sakir
supposed	ætla, ætluðu	souls	sáluhjápar, sálum
settled	bjó, bjóðast, björg, bjóst	same	sama, saman
strengthened	efldur	sat	sat, satt, sáttarfund, sáttarfundinum, sáttargerð
self-will	einræði		
still	enn, er, er	settlement	sáttargerð
sea	haf	say	segið, segir, segir
sea-going-ship	hafskip	says	segir
suitable	henta	send	senda
shoulders	herða	sent	sendi
sir	herra	set	sett, sett, setti
struck	hjó, hlaupa, hleypir	six	sex
satisfactory	hlítt	sinking	sígast
shrubs	hrísótt	sailed	sigldu
she	hún	Sigurd (name)	Sigurði, Sigurður
stormy	hvasst	Simon (name)	Símon, Símonar, símoni
seals	innsiglum	Simon's (name)	Símoni
son-of-Kalf (name)	Kálfsson	sit	sitja
son-of-Kodran (name)	Koðránsson	see	sjá
said	kvað, kvaðst, kváðu, kváðu, kváðust, kveðst, kveld, kyrrrlátir, kyrrt, Landeyjum, landi, landið, landsins	separated	skildu
		ship	skip, skipa, skipi
		ships	skips, skips
		Skjalgsbud (place)	Skjálgsbúða
		shortly	skjótlega
saying	kváðu	should-be	skyldi, skyldir
seek	leita, leysti	slipped	slæst
support	liðveislu	such	slík, slíka, slíkan, slíks, slíkt, slíku, slíkum
spoke	mælti, mæltu, mal		
sides	megin	strike	slógu
should	mun, mun, mun, mun, muna, mundi, mundu	small-ships	smáskipum
		sleep	sofa
shall-you	muntu	slept	sofnaði
shall	munu, munu, munu, munum, náðu	saga	sögu
		Sokki (name)	Sokka, Sokkason
son-of-Njal (name)	Njálsson	son-of-Sokki (name)	Sokkason
some	nokkuð, nokkur, nokkura, nokkurar, nokkurn, nokkurra, nokkuru, nokkurum	Solarfjoll (place)	Sólarfjöllum
		son	son
		sang	söng
something	nokkurra	sprang	spretta
swiftly	ört	stand	stað, staðar, staðarins
slander	róg	stood	staðið, stakk, standa
saw	sá, sá, sá, sægarpur	stepped	steig
so	sá, sá, sægarpur	stone-one	steinda
sea-champion	sægarpur	Steingrim's (name)	Steingríms
sought	sækja, Sæmundi		

115

Word List (English to Old Icelandic)

English	Old Icelandic	English	Old Icelandic
Steingrim (name)	Steingrímur	to	á, að, að, að, að, aðrir, áðu
stone-carving	steint	the-storm	andviðri
Steinthor (name)	Steinþór	the-Easterner	austmanns, austmanns
standing	stendur, sterkur	the-dwelling	bænum
strong	sterkur	throat	barkann
sitting-room	stofuna	the-boat	bátinn
seat	stól	the-bishop	biskuð, biskup, biskupi, biskups
supported	stutt		
steersman	stýrimaður, stýrimanns	the-bishop's	biskups
supporter	styrktarmaður	the-bishop-elect	biskupsefni
south	suður	the-bishop's-seat	biskupsstólinum, biskupsstólnum
summer	sumarið, sumars		
summers	sumur	the-trunk	bol
swear	sverji	the-tables	borð, borðið
skins	svörð	the-table	borðið
sleepy	syfjar	the-slope	brekku, brekkunni
showed	sýndi, sýndist	the-armour	brynjunni
seemed	sýndist	the-settlement	byggðina
sing	syngja	the-day	dag
sung	syngja	the-dead	daun
seems	sýnist, sýnt, systurson	the-court	dómi, dóminum
shown	sýnt	the-judgement	dómurinn
sister's-son	systurson	the-dream	drauminn
straightaway	þegar	the-animal	dýrið
straight-away	þegar	the-boat-behind	eftirbáti
servants-of	þjónustumenn	the-after-boat	eftirbátinn
son-of-Thord (name)	Þórðarson	than	en
son-of-Thorri (name)	Þórisson	then	er, er, er, er, er, er, er, erkibiskup
son-of-Thorljot (name)	Þorljótsson		
strange	undarlegt	the-archbishop	erkibiskup
submit	undir	they-are	eru, eru
solution	úrræði, úrræðið	travel	færu, færum, fagra, fallinn
should-they	væri		
slain	vegna	the-fairest	fagra
slaying	víg	to-catch	fangið
supplies	vistir	the-ferry	ferjuna
spring	vor, vor	the-fjord	fjörðu
		travelled	fór, fór, forn
		through	fyrir, fyrir
		to-do	gera, gera
		to-give	gera

T, t

English	Old Icelandic	English	Old Icelandic
that	á, á, á, að, að, að, að, aðrir, áðu, æðimaður, æpa, ætla	*treasure*	gersemi, gildur, gilla
		the-Greenlanders'	grænlendinga
		the-Greenlanders	grænlendingar
the	á, á, að, að, að, að, aðrir, áðu	*the-Greenlander*	grænlendings

Word List (English to Old Icelandic)

English	Old Icelandic	English	Old Icelandic
the-artefact-fee	gripagjaldið	the-men	mönnum
to-hold	halda	the-night	nætur, nátt
the-crew	hásetar	taking	nema
the-Hermunds (name)	Hermundur	the-unsettled-land	óbyggðum
things	hlutum	the-words	orðinn
they-had	höfðu	to-us	oss
to-strike	höggva	tore-up	rufu, sá
to-him	honum	together	saman, sami
time	hríð, hrinda	the-same	samt
the-branch	hríslunni	the-truth	sanni
thought	hugðu, hún, hurðina	truthfully	sannlegast
the-door	hurðina, hvað	true-words	sannyrði
turn	hverfa	true	
think	hygg	the-seam	sauminn
the-merchants	kaupmenn	this	sé, sé, segið, segir, segir, segir, segja, sektir, senda
the-trading-men	kaupmenn, kaupmenn, kaupmennirnir		
trading-men	kaupmenn, kaupmennirnir	to-be	sé, segið, segir
		to-be-sent	sendilegastan
teaching	kennimanns	them	sér, sér, sett, sett, sett
the-old-woman	kerlingu	themselves	sér, sett
the-keel	kilinum	theirs	sín, sína, sína, sinn, sinna, sinni, sínu
the-church	kirkju, kirkjuna		
the-king	konung, konungi, konungi, konungs	their	sína, sína
the-kind	konungi	they	sinni, sínu, sínum, sitja, sitt
the-king's	konungs		
the-king's-brief	konungsbréfum	the-cabin	skálann, skálann
the-Landeys (place)	Landeyjum	the-hut	skálann
the-land	landi, landið	temper	skaplyndi
the-lands	landsins	temperament	skapraun
the-way	leið	the-ships	skipa, skipi
team	lið, liði	the-ship	skipi, skipið, skipið, skipinu
the-body	lík, líkhringinguna		
the-funeral-procession	líkhringinguna	the-false-deacon	slembidjákn
told	mælt, mælti, mælti, mæltu	turned	snerist
		the-place	staðarins
the-matter	mal, mál, mál, máli, málið	thrust	stakk
		to-stand	standist
the-case	mál, mál	to-the-south	sunnan
the-matter-fulfilling	málsfyllingar	the-company	sveit
the-man	mann	to-the-sword	sverði
this-man	manninum	take	taka, taka
to-me	mér	took	taka, taki, tala
the-most	mestur	taken	tekið, tekinn, tekna, teknir
the-middle	miðju	thanked	þakkaði

Word List (English to Old Icelandic)

English	Old Icelandic
that-way	þannig
there	þar
those	þau
to-them	þeim
to-you	þér
these	þessi, þessi, þessir
the-assembly	þings
though	þó, Þóarinn
Thorarin (name)	Þóarinn, Þórarinn
Thord (name)	Þórðar, Þórðarson
Thord's (name)	Þórði
Thorfin (name)	Þorfinns
Thorgils (name)	Þorgils
Thori (name)	Þóris
third	þriðja
thirdly	þriðja
three	þrír, þrjá
the-more-difficult	þunglegar
therefore	því
the-service	tíða
tidings	tíðindi
the-news	tíðindin
tens	tigi, tigir
tent	tjald
tent-up	tjalda
twelve	tólf
time-like	tómlega
trust	traust
tread	troða
two	tveim, tvö
the-feast	veislunni
the-trees	viðinn
the-field	völlinn

U, u

English	Old Icelandic
upset	brugðið
unheard-of	endemi
use	nytjum
uncompensated	óbættur
un-settled	óbyggðir
un-equal	ójafnað
unequal	ójafnaður
unsettled	ósett
us	oss, Össur, Össurar
ungraceful	óþekktarsvip
un-worthy	óvirðing
uncertain	óvíst
uproar	róstu
unhappy	þungt
until	til
under	undir
up	upp, uppgefnir
up-given	uppgefnir
unable	vanfær

V, v

English	Old Icelandic
valid	gildur
very	mjög
violence	ofsa
victory	sigur
voiced	tjáði
Vestribyggd (place)	Vestribyggð, Vestribyggðar
Vighvats (name)	Víghvats

W, w

English	Old Icelandic
way	burt
while	en, endemi
was	er, er, er, er, er
we-are	er, er
what	er, er
when	er, er
where	er, er, er
who	er, er
with	er, erkibiskup, eru
were	eru, færu, færum
weak	fallinn, fang
went	fara, fara, fastmæli, fé, féið, fékk, feng, fengju, fer, ferjuna
wealth	fé, féið
would-get	fengju
wealth-finding	fjárfundinn
willing	fúsari
walked	gengið
was-named	hét

Word List (English to Old Icelandic)

English	Old Icelandic	English	Old Icelandic
white-bear	hvítabjörn	you	þér, þess, þessa, þessi, þessi
which	hvors		
whether	hvort	your	þín, þína
will	mun, mun, mun	yours	þína, þings
will-be	mun		
would	mun, muna, mundi, mundu, mundu, mundu, mundum, muni, muni		
would-be	mundu, mundum		
word	orð		
words	orð, orða		
word-sending	orðsending		
wandered	reikaði		
wounded	sárir		
went-away	stukku		
walrus-tusks	tannvöru		
washed	þvo		
worshippers	tíðamanni		
wool-comb	ullkamb		
win	unna		
weights	vættir		
weariness	varist		
wares	varning		
weather	veður		
well	vel		
willed	veld, vér, vér, vér		
we	vér, vér		
work	verk		
western	vestan		
winter	veturinn		
widely	víða		
wish	vil, vildi		
wanted	vildi		
wished-for	vilja		
wildly	villt		
worthiness	virðing, virðingar, virðum		
wise	vitrum, vitur		
wise-like	viturlega		
weaponed	vopnaðir		
with-you	yðvarn		

Y, y

A Word Comparison of Old Norse and Old Icelandic Words

Old Norse	Old Icelandic	English
áðr	áður	after
áðr	áður	before
æðimaðr	æðimaður	of-mind
aflat	aflað	gain
aftr	aftur	back
allmjök	allmjög	all-great
annat	annað	another
annat	annað	anything-else
annat	annað	other
annat	annað	otherwise
annathvárt	annaðhvort	other-either
Arnaldr	Arnaldur	Arnald (name)
at	að	a
at	að	at
at	að	by
at	að	in
at	að	it
at	að	of
at	að	that
at	að	the
at	að	to
auðit	auðið	possible
austmaðr	austmaður	Eastern-man
bændr	bændur	farmers
betr	betur	better
bezt	best	best
Bjarna	Bjarnar	Bjarn (name)
boðit	boðið	offering
bolöx	bol	the-trunk
borðit	borðið	bore-up
borðit	borðið	the-table
borit	borið	borne
borit	borið	brought
borit	borið	presented
Brandr	Brandur	Brand (name)
brögð	brang	chest
brotit	brotið	broken
brott	burt	away
brott	burt	way
brottu	burtu	away
brugðit	brugðið	upset
búit	búið	prepared
búit	búið	settled
búnaðr	búnaður	equipment
byrrinn	byrinn	bearing
byskup	biskuð	the-bishop
byskup	biskup	a-bishop
byskup	biskup	bishop
byskup	biskup	the-bishop
byskupi	biskupi	the-bishop
byskups	biskups	bishop
byskups	biskups	the-bishop
byskups	biskups	the-bishop's
byskupsefni	biskupsefni	the-bishop-elect
byskupslaust	biskupslaust	bishop-less
byskupsstólinum	biskupsstólinum	the-bishop's-seat
byskupsstóll	biskupsstóll	bishop's-seat
byskupsstólnum	biskupsstólnum	the-bishop's-seat
byskupsstólsins	biskupsstólsins	bishop's-seat
byskupsvígslu	biskupsvígslu	bishop's-appointment
dæmði	dæmdi	judged
Danmarkar	Danmerkur	Denmark (place)
dauðr	dauður	dead
dómr	dómur	judgement
dómrinn	dómurinn	the-judgement
dreymði	dreymdi	dreamed
dýrit	dýrið	the-animal
efldr	efldur	strengthened
einangr	einangur	alone-going
Einarr	Einar	Einar (name)
ek	eg	I
ekki	eigi	not

A Word Comparison of Old Norse and Old Icelandic

Old Norse	Old Icelandic	English
er	á	in
er	en	as
er	og	and
erendi	erindi	errand
erendis	erindis	errand
erkibyskup	erkibiskup	the-archbishop
erkibyskups	erkibiskups	archbishop
færi	færu	travel
færim	færum	travel
fáliga	fálega	coolly
fangit	fangið	to-catch
farim	förum	go
farit	farið	going
féit	féið	wealth
fekk	fékk	got
fekk	fékk	went
fell	féll	fell
fengi	fengju	would-get
ferlig	ferleg	fair
ferr	fer	went
féván	févon	fee-trust
frændr	frændur	kinsmen
framkvæmð	framkvæmd	execution
fundit	fundið	found
fylgði	fylgdi	follow
fylgði	fylgdi	followed
fylgðinni	fylgdinni	following
gefizt	gefist	given
gengit	gengið	been
gengit	gengið	going
gengit	gengið	walked
gengr	gengur	went
gera	geri	make
gerzt	gerst	done
gildr	gildur	valid
góðr	góður	good
grænlenzk	grænlensk	Greenlandic (name)
grænlenzkr	grænlenskur	a-Greenlander
grænlenzkum	grænlenskum	Greenlandic (name)
greiðist	greiðast	paying
gripagjaldit	gripagjaldið	the-artefact-fee
hafa	hefir	has-been
hagr	hagur	handy
haldit	haldið	holding
Hallr	Hallur	Hall (name)
hefði	hefðu	had
heimamaðr	heimamaður	house-man
heimilisprestr	heimilisprestur	local-priest
heldr	heldur	rather
heldu	héldu	held
hendr	hendur	hand
Hermundr	Hermundur	Hermund (name)
Hermundr	Hermundur	the-Hermunds (name)
hézt	hést	promised
hingat	hingað	here
hleypr	hleypur	ran
höfðaskipit	höfðaskipið	head-ship
höggvit	hoggið	struck
hringði	hringdi	called
hugr	hugur	mind
hvárirtveggja	hvorirtveggju	either-side
hvárirtveggju	hvorirtveggju	either-side
hvárrtveggi	hvortveggji	each
hvárs	hvors	which
hvárt	hvort	each
hvárt	hvort	whether
hváru	hvoru	each
hvárum	hvorum	each
hvat	hvað	that
hvat	hvað	what
hverr	hver	each
hverr	hver	who
inn	hinn	the
inu	hinu	the
Ísa-Steingrímr	Ísa-Steingrímur	Isa-Steingrim (name)
it	hið	the
it	hið	then
kaupskipit	kaupskipið	merchant-ship

A Word Comparison of Old Norse and Old Icelandic

Old Norse	Old Icelandic	English	Old Norse	Old Icelandic	English
kippðu	kipptu	pulled	mikit	mikið	great
kippim	kippum	jerk	mikit	mikið	many
klerkr	klerkur	cleric	mikit	mikið	much
komit	komið	come	mjök	mjög	much
kómu	komu	came	mjök	mjög	very
kómust	komust	came	morgininn	morguninn	morning
konungr	konungur	the-king	mun	minna	less
kostr	kostur	choice	mundi	mundu	would
kveðit	kveðið	declared	muni	munu	shall
kveðst	kvaðst	said	munu	mun	may
kyrrlátir	kyrrrlátir	still	myndim	mundum	would
lagðr	lagður	laid	nætr	nætur	night
landit	landið	the-land	nætr	nætur	the-night
leggr	leggur	propose	niðr	niður	down
legit	legið	laid	nökkur	nokkur	some
lengr	lengur	longer	nökkura	nokkura	some
leynivági	leynivogi	hidden-creek	nökkurar	nokkurar	some
lézt	lést	had	nökkurn	nokkurn	some
liðit	liðið	passed	nökkurra	nokkurra	something
líðr	líður	passed	nökkuru	nokkuru	some
liðveizlu	liðveislu	support	nökkurum	nokkurum	some
líkendi	líkindi	alike	nökkut	nokkuð	some
líkhringingina	líkhringinguna	the-funeral-procession	Nóreg	Noreg	Norway (place)
líkligast	líklegast	likely	nóregi	noregi	Norway (place)
lítit	lítið	little	Nóregs	Noregs	Norway (place)
lízt	líst	behold	óbættr	óbættur	uncompensated
Lundi	Lund	Lund (place)	ófúss	ófús	reluctant
lýkr	lýkur	ends	ójafnaðr	ójafnaður	unequal
maðr	maður	a-man	ok	og	also
maðr	maður	man	ok	og	and
mætti	mættu	might	ómegðarmaðr	ómegðarmaður	poor-man
makligast	maklegast	most	ór	úr	from
málahlutr	málahlutur	matter-lot	ór	úr	out-from
málit	málið	the-case	ór	úr	out-of
málum"	málum	cases	orðit	orðið	become
mánaðarmótit	mánaðarmótið	month's-end	orðit	orðið	have-become
mannvænlegr	mannvænlegur	a-friendly	órræði	úrræði	solution
margt	mart	many	órræðit	úrræðið	solution
mestr	mestur	the-most	ósæmð	ósæmd	dishonourable
mik	mig	me			
mikit	mikið	a-great			

A Word Comparison of Old Norse and Old Icelandic

Old Norse	Old Icelandic	English
óþekkðarsvip	óþekktarsvip	dishonourable
óþekkðarsvip	óþekktarsvip	ungraceful
Özur	Össur	Ossur (name)
Özurar	Össurar	of-Ossur (name)
Özurar	Össurar	Ossur (name)
Özuri	Össuri	Ossur (name)
Özurr	Össur	Ossur (name)
ráðligt	ráðlegt	advisable
reiðisvipr	reiðisvipur	angry
reiðr	reiður	angry
réttligast	réttlegast	correctness
sá	sáu	saw
sægarpr	sægarpur	sea-champion
sæmð	sæmd	honour
sæmðar	sæmdar	honour
sæmðir	sæmdir	honour
sakar	sakir	sake
sannligast	sannlegast	truthfully
sé	séu	are
sé	séu	they-are
sekðir	sektir	penalty
sendiligstan	sendilegastan	to-be-sent
settr	settur	set
sigr	sigur	victory
Sigurðr	Sigurður	Sigurd (name)
sik	sig	him
sik	sig	himself
skáladyrrnar	skáladyrnar	the-door
skilðu	skildu	parted
skilðu	skildu	separated
skipit	skipið	ship
skipit	skipið	the-ship
skjótliga	skjótlega	shortly
skulu	mun	would
skyldi	skyldu	should
skyli	skuli	shall
slátrgripa	sláturgripa	carcasses
sonr	son	son
staðit	staðið	stood
Steingrímr	Steingrímur	Steingrim (name)
Steinþórr	Steinþór	Steinthor (name)
stendr	stendur	standing
sterkr	sterkur	strong
stýrimaðr	stýrimaður	steersman
styrkðarmaðr	styrktarmaður	supporter
suðr	suður	south
sumarit	sumarið	summer
svá	svo	so
sveri	sverji	swear
sviptr	sviptur	deprived
svívirðliga	svívirðlega	disgracefully
systursonr	systurson	sister's-son
taka	taki	take
tekit	tekið	taken
þakði	þakti	covered
þangat	þangað	from-then
þangat	þangað	from-there
þat	það	it
þat	það	that
þat	það	the
þat	það	this
þat	það	to
þeira	þeirra	of-them
þeira	þeirra	theirs
þeira	þeirra	them
þeira	þeirra	they
þeirar	þeirrar	their
þessi	þessu	this
þik	þig	you
Þórðr	Þórður	Thord (name)
þóttumst	þóttist	thought
þungligar	þunglegar	the-more-difficult
þvá	þvo	washed
þykkir	þykir	seems
þykkist	þykist	seems
tíðenda	tíðinda	news
tíðendi	tíðindi	news
tíðendi	tíðindi	tidings
tíðendin	tíðindin	the-news
tíðendum	tíðindum	news

A Word Comparison of Old Norse and Old Icelandic

Old Norse	Old Icelandic	English
tómliga	*tómlega*	time-like
torsóttligt	*torsóttlegt*	difficult
tvau	*tvö*	two
týnzt	*týnst*	lost
undarligt	*undarlegt*	strange
vænlig	*vænleg*	hopeful
ván	*von*	expect
ván	*von*	expected
ván	*von*	hope
vanfærr	*vanfær*	unable
vanizt	*vanist*	custom
vápnaðir	*vopnaðir*	weaponed
vár	*vor*	spring
vár	*vor*	us
várit	*vorið*	spring
várkunn	*vorkunn*	pity
várn	*vorn*	our
várn	*vorn*	ours
varnarmaðr	*varnarmaður*	defender
várr	*vor*	our
várr	*vor*	ours
várri	*vorri*	ours
váru	*voru*	was
váru	*voru*	were
veðr	*veður*	weather
veizlu	*veislu*	feast
veizlunni	*veislunni*	the-feast
veldr	*veldur*	brought-about
veldr	*veldur*	caused
verðr	*verður*	becomes
verit	*verið*	been
vetrinn	*veturinn*	winter
vígit	*vígið*	killing
vildi	*vildu*	willed
virðim	*virðum*	worthiness
virðr	*virður*	respected
vistaföng	*vistföng*	resources
vit	*við*	with
vitr	*vitur*	wise
vitrliga	*viturlega*	wise-like
yðr	*yður*	you
yrði	*yrðu*	be

www.ingramcontent.com/pod-product-compliance
Lightning Source LLC
Chambersburg PA
CBHW051418070526
44584CB00023B/3476